CHRISTIAN WORLDVIEW

CHRISTIAN WORLDVIEW

Herman Bavinck

TRANSLATED AND EDITED BY

Nathaniel Gray Sutanto, James Eglinton,
and Cory C. Brock

WHEATON, ILLINOIS

Originally published in Dutch as *Christelijke wereldbeschouwing*, first edition by Bos in 1904, second edition by Kok in 1913, and third edition by Kok in 1929. This book is a translation of the second edition, which is in the public domain.

Cover Design: Jordan Singer

First printing 2019

Printed in the United States of America

Scripture quotations are drawn from the author's own translation of the Greek.

Hardcover ISBN: 978-1-4335-6319-5
ePub ISBN: 978-1-4335-6322-5
PDF ISBN: 978-1-4335-6320-1
Mobipocket ISBN: 978-1-4335-6321-8

Library of Congress Cataloging-in-Publication Data

Names: Bavinck, Herman, 1854–1921, author. | Sutanto, Nathaniel Gray, 1991–, editor.
Title: Christian worldview / Herman Bavinck ; translated and edited by Nathaniel Gray
    Sutanto, James Eglinton, and Cory C. Brock.
Other titles: Christelijke wereldbeschouwing. English
Description: Wheaton : Crossway, 2019. | Includes bibliographical references and index.
Identifiers: LCCN 2018046329 (print) | LCCN 2018047966 (ebook) | ISBN 9781433563201
    (pdf) | ISBN 9781433563218 (mobi) | ISBN 9781433563225 (epub) | ISBN
    9781433563195 (hc)
Subjects: LCSH: Christianity—Philosophy.
Classification: LCC BR100 (ebook) | LCC BR100 .B37513 2019 (print) | DDC 230.01—dc23
LC record available at https://lccn.loc.gov/2018046329

Crossway is a publishing ministry of Good News Publishers.

LB		28	27	26	25	24	23	22	21	20	19
15	14	13	12	11	10	9	8	7	6	5	4	3	2	1

Contents

Acknowledgments

This project could not have come to fruition without the generous help of many. First of all, we would like to thank Jonathan Gibson for his enthusiasm for this volume and for putting us in touch with Crossway. Thanks are also due to Justin Taylor and Jill Carter at Crossway for overseeing this work and for their commitment to bringing this project to completion.

In addition to his often-difficult Dutch syntax, Herman Bavinck also lavishly adorns his prose with German, Latin, and other foreign phrases or citations. Hence, many others were consulted to aid in the translating process. For their help in this regard, we would like to thank Michael Bräutigam, Ulrich Schmiedel, Nicholas Adams, Dolf te Velde, Ekke Oosterhuis and Mathilde Oosterhuis-Blok, Bram van den Heuvel, and especially the abundantly patient Marinus de Jong.

Gray Sutanto: I would like to thank the session and staff of Covenant City Church for their patience and willingness to permit me the time to undertake this task—

Tezar Putra, Elius Pribadi, Brett Bonnema, Jackie Burns, Emily Hendradjaja, and Tiffany Wijaya. It is a delight to labor with such a wonderful team. I am grateful, too, to my fiancée (at the time of writing), Indita Probosutedjo, for her patience, care, and love; to my parents, Leo Sutanto and Elly Yanti Noor; to my sisters, Novi, Mitzy, and Cindy Christina; and to my brothers-in-law, Aryo Kresnadi and Adriansyah Sukandar. God's providence and care often become tangible by means of their presence.

James Eglinton: I am grateful to Gray Sutanto and Cory Brock for their invitation to join this exciting translation project.

Cory Brock: Thanks are due to First Presbyterian Church Jackson for allowing me time to complete this work in the early days of ministry there. And, for Gray and me, James's expertise has been invaluable in the completion of the project, and special acknowledgment is due to him.

We acknowledge all mistakes and shortcomings as our own.

Gray Sutanto, James Eglinton, and Cory Brock
Jakarta, Edinburgh, and Jackson
September 2018

Editors' Introduction

Herman Bavinck for the Twenty-First Century

Since the recent English translation of his *Reformed Dogmatics* (2003–2008), Herman Bavinck (1854–1921)—the chief dogmatician of the Dutch Reformed tradition in the late nineteenth and early twentieth centuries—has gained a wide hearing among theologians in the twenty-first century. Bavinck was born into the orthodox Reformed tradition stemming from the 1834 Secession (*Afscheiding*) within the Dutch Reformed Church, a tradition committed simultaneously to Protestant orthodoxy and to the articulation of that orthodoxy in the rapidly changing cultural environs of the late modern Netherlands.

The cultural experience common to modern Europeans—Bavinck included, by implication—was marked by constant social, intellectual, technological, cultural, and spiritual upheaval. T. C. W. Blanning memorably describes that generation's ever-present awareness that "the ground [was] moving beneath their feet."[1] Bavinck, a professor of systematic theology at the Theological School in Kampen and then (at the time of writing this work) at the Free University of Amsterdam, wrote this treatise as a theologian addressing his constantly changing late modern world. The ideas found in this book were first aired in a rectorial address in Amsterdam in 1904. That address was immediately published and sold quickly. An expanded second edition was printed in 1913, with a third (posthumously released, otherwise unchanged) edition appearing in 1927. It is also worth noting that he intended his 1908 Stone Lectures, published as *Philosophy of Revelation*, to be a kind of sequel that further elaborated on the ideas in this work.[2] This volume, *Christian Worldview*, is the first English translation of Bavinck's address to a world in the throes of profound change on every front.

Contours of a Christian Worldview

In Bavinck's context, the philosophy of Ernest Renan—with its spirit of scientific materialism—had dominated the late nineteenth century. Alongside this thinking, however, the youth of Zarathustra had failed: religion had not died, although the classic Christian religion was under

---

1. T. C. W. Blanning, introduction to *The Oxford Illustrated History of Modern Europe*, ed. Blanning (Oxford: Oxford University Press, 1996), 1.

2. Herman Bavinck, *Wijsbegeerte der Openbaring* (Kampen: Kok, 1908), 275n31. For a modern English translation, see *Philosophy of Revelation: A New Annotated Edition*, ed. Cory Brock and Gray Sutanto (Peabody, MA: Hendrickson, 2018), 23n61.

suspicion and despised. In this milieu, Bavinck began his book *Christelijke wereldbeschouwing*, or *Christian Worldview*, by noting the consequence of this "modern" problem: "Before all else, what strikes us in the modern age is the internal discord that consumes the self."[3] The corrupted consciousness of the human personality in the prevailing world, he argued, derives from the "aversion to the common Christian faith" and to historic religion in general.[4] While every human being is undeniably religious at heart, that era's denial of objective religion gave way to the awakening of a sickness in body and soul: the discord of the disordered personality. There is, then, Bavinck wrote in 1904, "a disharmony between our thinking and feeling, between our willing and acting. There is a discord between religion and culture, between science and life."[5]

The modern self, he argued, both disparages religion (feeling) at the hand of science (thinking) and desperately needs what it rejects. The modern will feels the weight of the moral order but acts in dissociation with its own deepest needs and desires. Herein, one finds a brief definition of *worldview*: it is an attempt to unify the self, the head and heart, on the ground of a primary agreement between religion, science, and philosophy. A world-and-life view means, in brief, faith seeking understanding. It is important to note that Bavinck's preferred term is

3. See p. 22 below. In this editors' introduction, quotations from Bavinck's *Christian Worldview* are cited by page number within this volume.
4. See p. 24 below.
5. See p. 22 below.

world-and-life view, rather than merely *worldview*. In a world-and-life view, the term *world* refers to the objective domain, reality outside the self; the term *life* refers to the human subject, the consciousness and its needs, desires, knowledge, and affections. A unified world-and-life view seeks justification for the unity between the subjective and objective. And at the dawn of the twentieth century, Bavinck argued, "A 'unified' [*einheitliche*] world-and-life view is lacking, and therefore this word is the slogan of our day."[6]

For this reason, in a significant adaptation of Immanuel Kant's (1724–1804) notion of the *Anschauungen* ("intuitions"), Bavinck's and Abraham Kuyper's (1837–1920) *wereldbeschouwing* helped birth the contemporary use of the concept *Christian worldview*. The Christian *wereldbeschouwing* uniquely addresses several fundamental questions that all worldviews must face and offers a derivative thesis:

> What is the relation between thinking and being, between being and becoming, and between becoming and acting? What am I? What is the world, and what is my place and task within this world? Autonomous thinking finds no satisfactory answer to these questions—it oscillates between materialism and spiritualism, between atomism and dynamism, between nomism and antinomianism. But Christianity pre-

---

6. See p. 22 below.

serves the harmony [between them] and reveals to us a wisdom that reconciles the human being with God and, through this, with itself, with the world, and with life.[7]

These questions are shorthand for substantial topics in the spheres of philosophy and theology, the types of questions that impose themselves on every thoughtful individual at some point. The first aforementioned pairing (between thinking and being), for example, concerns epistemology. How do I know that I see reality as it truly is? Or, more appropriately, how do I know that the reality I experience is trustworthy? The second pair (between being and becoming) is a veiled reference to how identity relates to change. How can we account for identity across time, or for a unity of essence in the midst of a multiplicity and even disparity of parts? Third, the pairing of becoming and acting refers to the questions of ethics. How should I live? What is good? Individuals seeking a coherence of head and heart combine questions like these, alongside the cosmogonic and teleological, to form a world-and-life view.

But how so? How, for Bavinck, does worldview arise? The reader will find no single definition or singular thesis for worldview or worldview formation within this treatise. Rather, one must cobble together regular phrases, synonyms, and implicit explanations. In the first chapter, Bavinck helpfully parses the common route the individual

---

7. See p. 29 below.

takes to arrive at a worldview. One might begin there, with the path to knowing an all-inclusive reality, the physical and metaphysical. Also, similar terms to worldview do abound. Worldview is (at least) closely related to a "comprehensive wisdom"[8] or, in the case of a particularly Christian worldview, to a "Christian wisdom."[9] Nevertheless, for Bavinck, wisdom and worldview are not mere synonyms: "Whoever rejects the word of the Lord cannot have wisdom."[10] (In that regard, this text provides an interesting counterpoint to the recent trend in Anglophone Reformed theology to pit worldview against wisdom, as though the former were a largely cerebral affair, in contrast to the wholesome embodied nature of the latter.)

Each individual, Bavinck argues, is first addressed by the world through means of sensation. These sensations birth concepts—concepts that correspond to the world of being. We experience, we judge, we learn, and we gather. These experiences beget the search for truth, for metaphysics. Metaphysical awareness, like wisdom in its most historical sense, does not arise a priori. The "results of science are and remain the starting point of philosophy."[11] Wisdom, or philosophy, aims above the sciences. It seeks the truth where it can be found. It unifies and "press[es] through" to the first principles.[12] It

8. See p. 48 below.
9. See p. 52 below.
10. See p. 39 below.
11. See p. 50 below.
12. See p. 50 below.

traces "leading ideas" within the domains of philosophical thought and finds their common place.[13] Wisdom seeks the "idea of the whole in the parts," and when it discovers it, one finds there not only the unifying principle of philosophy but also the ground of religion.[14] Comprehensive wisdom seeks to know reality as a whole, as it truly is, and to know all that it demands. A world-and-life view arises here—where one obtains a vision for the final ground of all things, wherein all the domains of knowledge cohere, where the primary cause both explains and gives life, and where religion comes to bear on that comprehensive wisdom, unveiling the same primary cause for all life.

Worldview, for Bavinck, is neither apriorism nor a tenuous theory for separating public intellectuals into neat compartments. Rather, it is a controlling principle and posture that is first discovered when religion comes to bear on both science and wisdom (philosophy), discovering between them a unity—one which attempts to satisfy both head and heart. Citing Friedrich Adolf Trendelenburg, Bavinck argues that wisdom stems from and leads to a worldview, "because it is indeed the 'science of the idea' [*Wissenschaft der Idee*]."[15] Wisdom is possible because the world was first freely known by divine wisdom. Since religion is inescapable, in Bavinck's view, even the materialist holds to a world-and-life view that is both

---

13. See p. 50 below.
14. See p. 51 below.
15. See p. 51 below.

religious and scientific, a matter of faith and fact. Even when considering nothing more than sense perception, the revelation of God speaks and says to the personality, "Look up and see." It is only the Christian worldview that provides true harmony of self: true harmony between God and the world, God and the self, and the self and the world.

To put it otherwise, Bavinck offers a threefold frame for thinking about how we think. First, science in general arises from our observation and judgment making. We learn things about the real world. Second, based on our relation to this reality, we also make metaphysical judgments—we search for truth, both what is true and how to live truly, and this search is the discipline of wisdom. Finally, when wisdom, in search of a comprehensive unity, meets and bows to the demands of religion, in both its ontological and ethical demands, there is a world-and-life view. From there, one's world-and-life view does not remain static. Rather, it rereads the cosmos, the sensations, and the metaphysical claims and makes ongoing adjustments, always seeking the satisfaction of head and heart. It strives for subjective and objective unity. A worldview is a map, drawn over time from careful research, derived from actual knowledge of the geography, from pious religion, from the desire for truth, and it is amenable to updating. After all, maps are made from research—some careful, meticulous, and true and some not. Some maps account for the details as they are presented, and some are false. But map making we must do. Aside from the metaphor, a world-and-life view means that, over time and in engagement with reality as it presents itself, one has arrived at a basic, primary answer to the fundamental religious and philosophical questions of existence: What am I? Where did I come from? How does my mind relate to the world outside me? Do I, and how can I, know? How should I act? And what is the point of life? To where am I going?

In the treatise that follows, translated from the updated (1913) edition, Bavinck explains why only Christianity has solutions for the discordant self in the modern world, paying special attention to epistemology, change, and ethics. On the ground that God's grace restores and perfects nature, Bavinck argues that only Christianity can make sense of the deepest human needs while simultaneously "justif[ying]" the "presupposition[s]" from which we approach the objective world.[16] This is so, he argues, because Christ is the steward of creation and re-creation, of both nature and grace.

Note on the Text

The original Dutch text includes untranslated terms and phrases in German, Greek, Latin, and French. Instead of simply translating these phrases into English, we have indicated every instance in which Bavinck uses these foreign terms, since they often signal important sources

---

16. See p. 40 below.

for Bavinck. In that light, we present two classes of bracketed foreign terms in our translation: Dutch terms and non-Dutch foreign terms. First, we use brackets for Dutch terms because the original Dutch may prove helpful to English readers or may communicate a nuance that might otherwise be missed if the original were not provided. For the English translation of Dutch terms, we omit quotation marks to retain the sense that these terms were native to the original reader. Second, we bracket other foreign language terms and set the English translations for these in quotation marks, which signals that these terms were foreign to the original reader. In a few cases, the foreign terms seemed important enough to keep in the main text, so in those instances the English translation (rather than the foreign term) appears in brackets.

We have sought to maintain precision and to preserve the original meaning without sacrificing smoothness of English prose in this translation. In some cases we have added words where we felt that sentences, when rendered into English, would not make sense without them. Our goal is to make the text as accessible as possible, while also encouraging scholarly readers to study the original text in conjunction with this translation.

Preface to the Second Edition

The first edition of this *Christian Worldview*, which appeared in 1904, has been sold out for some time, and the publisher was of the opinion that a second edition would still be well received. For this reason, I meticulously read the treatise through once more and introduced some changes. In 1904, this work also served as a rectorial address, but because of its length, only a small segment was actually delivered; now [in its written form], all that would bring that address [in its shortened form] to memory is omitted. There are indeed changes here and there; in the text and especially in the notes, some clarifications and additions are included. Finally, to elevate the usefulness of this little book, I included a table of contents and an index at the end. May its reading greatly strengthen you in the faith, unto the truth and beauty of the Christian worldview.

H. Bavinck
Amsterdam, May 1913

Introduction

With the turn of the nineteenth to the twentieth century, many people of renown made daring attempts to determine the character of the centennial era that had just ended.[1] Although providing only an approximation, they attempted to do so in order to offer their opinion regarding the direction that the current of life was flowing.[2] But this field they were to survey was so extensive and the phenomena that drew their attention were so diverse, important, and complex that no one has been successful in summarizing that rapidly advancing century under a single formula or in defining the direction of the future with some singular character trait. While one person was looking for *the* character of the previous century in the awakening of the historical or natural sciences, others gave attention to the development of commerce, to the

---

1. Bavinck's original address dates to 1904.—Ed.
2. For example, see H. S. Chamberlain, *Die Grundlagen des neunzehnten Jahrhunderts* (München: Bruckman, 1904); Theobald Ziegler, *Die geistigen und socialen Strömungen des neunzehnten Jahrhunderts* (Berlin: Bondi, 1901); Ludwig Stein, *An der Wende des Jahrhunderts* (Freiburg: J. T. B. Mohr, 1899); Ernst Troeltsch, "Neunzehntes Jahrhundert," in *Realencyklopädie für protestantische Theologie und Kirche* (Graz: Akademische Druck- u. Verlagsanstalt, 1896–1913), 24:244–60.

significance of the creation of the machine, to the desire for emancipation, or to the development of democracy. And while some believed we were living in a time marked by neomysticism or neo-Romanticism, others decided that psychologism or relativism, autonomy or anarchy were better descriptions of the direction in which we were moving. Although truth may indeed be found in all these designations, none of them expresses the fullness of modern life.

This is so because, before all else, what strikes us in the modern age is the internal discord that consumes the self and the restless haste that drives it. The *fin de siècle* ["turn of the century"] is characterized as a period of dramatic change—although this is a designation that says little, because every time is a time of change. But the peculiarity of this moment is that everyone feels an epoch of change, when all people realize they cannot remain the same, and that some long for this moment to pass by more swiftly than others.[3] There is a disharmony between our thinking and feeling, between our willing and acting. There is a discord between religion and culture, between science and life. A "unified" [*einheitliche*] world-and-life view is lacking, and therefore this word is the slogan of our day.[4] The search for this concord is the work in which all who follow their era with interest participate.

3. Ziegler, *Die geistigen und socialen Strömungen*, 561.
4. On the origin and meaning of the word, see James Orr, *The Christian View of God and the World* (Edinburgh: Elliott, 1893), 1, 415; Albert Maria Weisz, *Die religiöse Gefahr* (Freiburg: Herder, 1904), 106.

Now that the "period of Renan" (with its scientific materialism, its religious modernism, its moral utilitarianism, its aesthetic naturalism, and its political liberalism) is no longer the spirit of the age, a younger generation has arisen that, disappointed in expectations that were awakened but not fulfilled, has again become tormented by the mysteries of being. A new generation has come to the fore, which has exchanged the insight that we have moved forward so gloriously far, for the appreciation that the unknowable and unrecognizable surrounds us on all sides. Alongside the ongoing idolization of science and culture on the one hand, a return to mystical idealism, to a vague belief in things unseen, which is influential in every field of study, can be perceived on the other. If we choose to, we can perceive both a shameless employment of bare egoism and a dedication to the community, which, even in its deranged ascetic and communistic forms, fills us with respect. In literature and art, the flattest realism is exchanged with love for the mysterious in nature and history and with the honoring of the symbolic. Here patriotism degenerates into narrow-minded chauvinism and, as a result, is sacrificed to a "humanity without fatherland." The place of the *milieu* theory and the notion of racial instinct[5] is challenged by hero worship, the cult of genius,

---

5. Here Bavinck refers to deterministic theories advanced in nineteenth-century Europe by the likes of Ernest Renan (1823–1892), who argued that instinctual racial characteristics determined behavioral traits, and Hippolyte Taine (1828–1893), who argued that genius was the product of both race and environment (*milieu*).—Ed.

and the apotheosis of the *Übermensch*.[6] Besides a historical sensibility, which glorifies all existence, we discover a
revolutionary impulse that despises the historical. Repris-
tination and emancipation wrestle with each other for the
plunder. Marx[7] and Nietzsche work together to curry the
public's favor. Between socialism and individualism, between democracy and aristocracy, between classicism and
Romanticism, between atheism and pantheism, between
unbelief and superstition, civilized humanity swings back
and forth.

Shared by both movements, nevertheless, is, undoubt-
edly, an aversion to the common Christian faith. While
one modern movement is indeed different from another,
what is clear is that historical Christianity has had its day.
It no longer fits with our Copernican worldview, or with
our knowledge of nature and her immutable laws, with
our modern culture, with our "this-worldliness" [*Dies-
seitigkeit*] outlook on life, with our valuation of material goods. The thought world of Scripture is no longer
embedded in our ways of thinking. The whole of Christianity, with its Trinity and incarnation, with its creation
and fall, with guilt and atonement, with heaven and hell,

---

6. Bavinck is referring to the "cult of genius" typical of much German Romanticism. In contrast to the aforementioned deterministic theories of behavior,
Romanticism celebrated the genius as one whose heroism was rooted in an ability
to transcend and break with laws and conventions. This view was represented by
Friedrich Schlegel (1772–1829), and the genius was celebrated as the "Superman"
(*Übermensch*) in the writings of Friedrich Nietzsche (1844–1900), a German philosopher who held significant influence over Western thought.—Ed.

7. Karl Marx (1818–1883) was a German philosopher and political theorist
whose writings shaped much of later socialist thinking.—Ed.

belongs in an obsolete worldview and is, accordingly, gone for good. It no longer speaks to our generation and is separated by a deep chasm from our modern consciousness and life. The "shibboleths" [*Schlagwörter*] "God," "soul," and "immortality," says Meyer-Benfey,[8] have lost their meaning for us. Who still feels the need today to dispute about God's existence? We no longer need God. There is no place for him in our world. Let the old hermit in the forest continue to worship God. We, the youth of Zarathustra, know that God is dead and will not be resurrected.[9]

The convergence of this rejection of Christianity and the inner discord that disturbs us in modern life gives occasion to the question whether the two phenomena exist in a causal relation. And this question is urgent when we see that at the demise of the Christian religion, no one can find comfort and everyone is fantasizing about the search for a new religion. Although there are thousands who confess with their mouths that not only Christianity but all religion is finished, the number of those who call for a new religion, a new dogma, and a new morality increases day by day. The age in which religion's day was thought to have passed flies swiftly by our eyes. The expectation that science, virtue, or art would make religion superfluous is entertained by few. It is precisely the loss

8. Heinrich Meyer-Benfey (1869–1945) was a German literary scholar.—Ed.

9. Heinrich Meyer-Benfey, *Moderne Religion* (Leipzig: Diederichs, 1902), 130. [Nietzsche's *Thus Spoke Zarathustra* was a philosophical novel that sets out the death of God and the emergence of the *Übermensch*.—Ed.]

of religion that gives rise to the inventors of new religions everywhere—and in great numbers. They are built up from the strangest and wildest elements. One goes to the school of Darwin and Haeckel, to Nietzsche and Tolstoy, to Hegel and Spinoza.[10] One sets off, on the basis of the histories of religious lands and peoples, in order to find what he wants in India and Arabia, in Persia and Egypt. One borrows elements from occultism and theosophy, from spiritism and magic. And everything is then made into an object of religious veneration, both world and humanity, heroes and geniuses, science and art, state and society, the world of spirits and the power of nature. Each has its own divinity. While it is not only [seen like] this, religion has become, for many, a private matter, which they arrange to their own liking. And yet they all hope to work toward a "betterment of religion" [*Weiterbildung der Religion*], toward a new religion yet to come, toward a "this-worldly religion" [*Diesseitsreligion*] and a "world religion" [*Weltreligion*] that can supersede and repair the supernatural and "other-worldly" [*jenseitige*] Christianity.[11]

---

10. Bavinck is referring to English naturalist and evolutionist Charles Darwin (1809–1882), German biologist and philosopher Ernst Haeckel (1834–1919), German philosopher Friedrich Nietzsche (1844–1900), Russian novelist Leo Tolstoy (1828–1910), German philosopher Georg Wilhelm Friedrich Hegel (1770–1831), and Jewish-Dutch philosopher Benedict de Spinoza (1632–1677).—Ed.

11. Weisz, *Die religiöse Gefahr*, 78–110; Engelbert Lorenz Fischer, *Die modernen Ersatzversuche für das aufgegebene Christentum* (Regensburg: Manz, 1902); E. Haach, *Die modernen Bemühungen um eine Zukunftsreligion* (Leipzig: Wallman, 1903); Pierre Daniel Chantepie de la Saussaye, "De godsdienst der wetenschap," *Onze Eeuw* (November 1904): 394–420; Theodor Simon, *Modern Surrogate für das Christentum* (Berlin: Hobbing, 1910); Pearson M'Adam Muir, *Modern Substitutes for Christianity*, Baird Lectures 1909 (London: Hodder and Stoughton, 1909);

The Christian religion views this seeking and groping of a corrupt humanity not with indifference but rather with a sublime peace and even a joyful certainty. Christianity stands antithetically to all that is brought before the market today under the name *religion*. If we understand Christianity's warrant and maintain a desire to preserve her essence, then we can do nothing else but take a resolute position against the systems of the day and the worldviews of its own invention and fashioning. There can be no question of "mediation" [*Vermittlung*]. There can be no thought of reconciliation. The times are too grave to flirt with the spirit of the age. The deep, sharp contrast standing between the Christian faith and the modern person[12] must provide us with the insights that picking portions of each is not possible and that deciding between alternatives is a duty. However lovely peace would be, the conflict is upon us.[13]

But there is no reason for despondency. The adversary supplies us the weapons in hand to combat him. When the reconciliation that Christianity offers is rejected, the above division, which abides in the human heart, inevitably comes to the surface. All disharmony in our being has its origin therein. That is, although

David Balsillie, *Is a World-Religion Possible?* (London: Griffiths, 1909). One thinks further still to the religious movement of the *Monistenbond*, the Order of the Eastern Star; of the Church of the New Thought; of the world religion of Tokonami, deputy minister of domestic affairs in Japan; of Annie Besant; of 'Abdu'l Bahá; etc.

12. Bartholomaus von Carneri, *Der moderne Mensch* (Stuttgart: Strauss, [ca. 1910]).

13. Ernst Gustav Steude, "Auf zum Kampfe," *Beweis des Glaubens* 40 (January 1904): 3–23.

we, according to the testimony of our conscience, are removed from God by our sin, we cannot do without his fellowship.[14] If we reject Christianity because it does not suit us, it instantly proves at the very same time that Christianity is indispensable for us. So when the world cries out, "Away with Christ," Christ shows precisely in his death that he alone gives life to the world. Christianity does not fit the deviant concepts that modern humanity forms about the world and life. It stands diametrically opposed to them. But there is a better fit between the world and life as they are in themselves. Whoever shakes off the idols of the day and knows to rise above the prevailing prejudices in science and the academy, who faces up to the things themselves, soberly and watchfully, and takes world and humanity, nature and religion as they truly are in themselves, presses on, evermore strengthening the conviction that Christianity is the only religion whose view of the world and life fits the world and life.[15] The idea of Christianity and the meaning of reality belong together like lock and key: they make sense together. This much is made somewhat clear by three problems addressed from ancient times, the questions that formed a world-and-life view then.

---

14. Cf. Paul Tillich, *Mystik und Schuldbewusstsein in Schellings philosophischer Entwicklung* (Gütersloh: Bertelsmann, 1912).

15. That Christianity, although not in itself a science or philosophy but a religion, implies a defined view of both world and life is clearly demonstrated in Orr, *Christian View*, 3–36.

In ancient Greece, philosophy, as academic study was known generally, was divided into dialectics, physics, and ethics. (These names can be amended to an extent or be exchanged for others, such as logic [noetics] and natural and mental philosophies, but all frameworks eventually come back to this older trilogy).[16] The problems that confront the human mind always return to these: What is the relation between thinking and being, between being and becoming, and between becoming and acting? What am I? What is the world, and what is my place and task within this world? Autonomous thinking finds no satisfactory answer to these questions—it oscillates between materialism and spiritualism, between atomism and dynamism, between nomism and antinomianism. But Christianity preserves the harmony [between them] and reveals to us a wisdom that reconciles the human being with God and, through this, with itself, with the world, and with life.

---

16. Eduard von Hartmann, *Philosophie des Unbewussten* (Leipzig: Haacke, 1904), 3:18.

1

Thinking and Being

This reconciliation occurs first in the light of the problem of thinking [*denken*] and being [*zijn*]. From ancient times onward, humanity has pondered how the mind [*geest*][1] in us can have consciousness of the things outside us and how the mind can know [*kennen*] them—in other words, what is the origin, the essence, and the limit of human knowledge [*kennis*]? The fact is certain that of ourselves and without coercion, we presume a world that exists outside us, that we seek to make it our mental property by way of perception and thinking [*denken*], and that acting thusly, we also suppose that we should obtain a

---

1. *Geest* has a wide semantic range and can refer to the mind, the spirit, or a ghost.—Ed.

certain and trustworthy knowledge of it. But on what grounds does this faith in a reality that is independent from our consciousness rest, and what guarantee is there that our consciousness—enriched through observation and thinking—corresponds to the world of being [*zijn*]?

For as long as the human being has occupied himself with this problem, he almost always ends up on one side or another, either sacrificing knowledge to being or being to knowledge. Empiricism trusts only sensible perceptions and believes that the processing of elementary perceptions into representations and concepts, into judgments and decisions, removes us further and further from reality and gives us only ideas [*denkbeelden*] that, though clean and subjectively indispensable, are merely "nominal" [*nomina*] and so are subjective representations, nothing but "the breath of a voice" [*flatus vocis*], bearing no sounds, only merely a "concept of the mind" [*conceptus mentis*]. Conversely, rationalism judges that sensible perceptions provide us with no true knowledge; they bring merely cursory and unstable phenomena into view, while not allowing us to see the essence of the things. Real, essential knowledge thus does not come out of sensible perceptions but comes forth from the thinking of the person's own mind; through self-reflection we learn the essence of things, the existence of the world.

In both cases and in both directions, the harmony between subject and object, and between knowing and being, is broken. With the former [i.e., empiricism], the world is nominalistically[2] divided into its parts; with the latter [i.e., rationalism], reality is hyper-realistically identified with the idea. In the former, the danger of sensualism and materialism threatens, and in the latter, that of idealism and monism. With both, the concept of truth, of "conformity of intellect and thing" [*conformitas intellectus et rei*], a correspondence between thinking and being, is lost. For in empiricism it falls together with the empirical, sensibly perceptible reality, and in rationalism it follows out on a correspondence between thoughts with themselves, on an internal clarity, on logical necessity. So in both directions the final question arises, whether there is truth, and [if so,] what it is.

Now, however, truth is the indispensable good for our cognition and thus the goal of all science [*wetenschap*]. If there is no truth, gone with that, too, is all knowledge and science. The Christian religion thus shows its wisdom primarily in this, that it knows and preserves truth as an objective reality, which exists independent of our consciousness and is displayed by God for us in his works of nature and grace. Accordingly, each person proceeds spontaneously on the basis of the conviction that the objective world exists outside him and that it exists as he has come to know it in clear perception. Doubt does not arise in him. Only when he later tries to give

---

2. "Nominalism," as used by Bavinck, refers to the philosophical view that there are no universal essences or abstract concepts in reality. It is the view, rather, that these abstract concepts are reducible to linguistic aids that serve pragmatic purposes.—Ed.

an account of the reasons and grounds on which he can proceed in such a manner can doubt emerge concerning the justification of his action. For first, the distinction and the distance between physical reality and psychical sensation is so great that it seems there can be no talk of a correspondence and concurrence between them. And another issue is that a spontaneous act of faith underlies the acceptance of the reality of an external world and our trust in the truth of sense perception, a faith whose scientific credentials cannot be proved under the scrutiny of the sharpest reflection. Here whoever does not want to begin with faith but demands sufficient proofs bars himself from the way of science and has set his foot on the slippery slope of skepticism.

This misstep has already been taken with the claim that we know nothing immediately beyond our own sensations [*gewaarwordingen*] and representations [*voorstellingen*]. Whosoever speaks this way has already been caught in the snares of idealism and cannot free himself by any reasoning: the very same reasoning would apply to all the evidences one would want to bring forward for the reality of the outside world and for the trustworthiness of sense perception. No law of cause and effect can release the one who accepts the principle and starting point of idealism from the Circassian Circle [*toovercirkel*][3]

---

3. The "Circassian Circle" was a folk dance wherein participants form a large circle through which they move, constantly changing partners throughout the progression of the dance.—Ed.

of his representations: out of one representation he can only deduce another, and he is never able to bridge the chasm between thinking and being by reasoning. Neither can voluntarism provide any service here. From the standpoint of idealism, the opposition that the will encounters turns the will itself into a representation. And will and opposition are then not two independent realities from my consciousness but two acts of consciousness [*bewustzijnsacten*] that stand in a certain relationship to each other. The idealism adopted in principle leaves no room for realism, even for critical and transcendental realism; no more proof is possible to show that the category of causality possesses transcendent validity, for such a category might well have strength in a world that exists but not in a world whose reality must first be proved.

None of this denies that the object can only become known by the subject and be known through thinking. No one can repudiate it, in the sense that a man cannot watch himself walk along a street and cannot stand up on his own shoulders. We know the external world only through our sensations and can never approach it from beyond them. The one who does not trust knowledge until he has been able to control that which is outside himself makes an impossible and absurd demand of knowing, precisely because knowing is always—and can never be other than—a relation between subject and object. As soon as one or both falls away, there is no more knowing.

But this acknowledgment, that knowledge of the object comes only through the subject, differs vastly from the idealistic assertion that the subject immediately knows only his own sensations and representations. Our sensations and representations first become the object, the immediate object of knowledge, when we devote ourselves to psychological studies and reflect on our own soul life [*zieleleven*]. But psychology is something other than "epistemology" [*Erkenntnisstheorie*]. If we perceive the world outside ourselves, then the sensations and representations we receive by it are not the *object* of our knowledge but the knowledge itself, which we have directly obtained through perception of the outside world. In the sensations, we have knowledge not of those sensations, at least not in the first place and not immediately, but of that which is sensed [*gewaargewordene*]. And out of the sensations, we do not deduce, by syllogisms, a world beyond ourselves, which then might not exist or which might exist wholly differently from what we perceive. But in the sensations, the objective world is given to us, and this is recognized and accepted by us, just as we perceive it.[4] Naturally, those sensations are often impure and imprecise; our senses are faulty, and our subjec-

---

4. Friedrich Adolf Trendelenburg, *Logische Untersuchungen* (Leipzig: Hirzel, 1862), 2:476; Engelbert Lorenz Fischer, *Die Grundfragen der Erkenntnisstheorie* (Mainz: Kirchheim, 1887), 240; Wilhelm Wundt, *Grundriss der Psychologie* (Leipzig: Engelmann, 1897), 52; Georg Theodor Ziehen, *Leitfaden der physiologischen Psychologie* (Jena: Fischer, 1900), 30; Johannes Reinke, *Die Welt als That* (Berlin: Paetel, 1903), 25, 97; Rudolf Eisler, *Wörterbuch der philosophischen Begriffe*, 2nd ed. (Berlin: Ernst Siegfried Mittler und Sohn, 1904), 1:269.

tivity also often exerts influence on perception. But this impurity and imprecision in our sensations, which can be remedied only through ever-repeated, rigorous perception, does not abrogate the conviction that in sensations and representations we possess a trustworthy knowledge of objective reality. Even the qualitative properties of things, such as colors and sounds, are, as currently again more commonly recognized, not to be explained merely out of an innate, specific energy of the senses but are also determined in part through the external stimuli on the nerves.[5]

This now is the fact that underpins all sensation and representation. He who denies it undermines all truth and science. He comes then with Nietzsche to the doctrine that subject and object are two absolutely different spheres, that in the act of knowing, the human person always gets in his own way and always veils things by his subjective sensations. The logical upshot is, then, to claim with the same philosopher that there is no world of being and no realm of truth; the apparent [*schijnbaar*] world is the only one, and the so-called "true" world is something that we make up. It is but a moral prejudice and an ascetic ideal that the truth has more worth than

5. James Orr, *David Hume and His Influence on Philosophy and Theology* (London: Hodder and Stoughton, 1903); Christoph Willems, *Die Erkenntnislehre des modernen Idealismus* (Trier: Paulinus, 1906); Richard Hönigswald, *Ueber die Lehre Humes von der Realität der Aussendinge* (Berlin: Schwetschke, 1907). Cf. Herman Bavinck, *Wijsbegeerte der Openbaring* (Kampen: Kok, 1908), 61ff. [For a modern English translation of this work, see Herman Bavinck, *Philosophy of Revelation: A New Annotated Edition*, ed. Cory Brock and Gray Sutanto (Peabody, MA: Hendrickson, 2018), 61ff.—Ed.]

the appearance. The only word of worth in the New Testament is Pilate's skeptical question: What is truth?[6]

Knowledge of truth is possible only if we begin with the fact that subject and object, and knowing and being, correspond to each other. This fact stands firmly in the immediate awareness of all people and is accepted—consciously or unconsciously—by all who still believe in truth and science. It is science's task to explain this fact, but if it cannot do this, it will then, on pain of suicide, have to leave the matter untouched. And it will be capable of explanation only if it allows itself to be illumined by the wisdom of the divine word [*Goddelijk Woord*], which sets on our lips the confession of God the Father, the Almighty, Creator of heaven and earth. This confession is not only the first article of our Christian faith but also the foundation and cornerstone of all knowledge and science. Only with this confession can one understand and uphold the harmony of subject and object, of thinking and being. The organs of our perception are thus connected to the elements, out of which the whole cosmos is composed, by virtue of a common origin, and so each

---

6. Friedrich Rittelmeyer, *Friedrich Nietzsche und das Erkenntnisproblem* (Leipzig: Engelman 1903), 6, 16, 33, 60–62. This is actually nothing other than the doctrine of the old Sophists, who called the human being the measure of all things. But recently this sophism has been renewed, though not in such a crass form as that of Nietzsche, mainly by the so-called pragmatism of William James, which is anti-intellectualist and seeks its mark of truth in the utility and productivity of knowledge. Joseph de Tonquédec, *La notion de vérité dans la Philosophie Nouvelle* (Paris: Beauchesne, 1908); August Deneffe, "Relative Wahrheit," *Stimmen aus Maria-Laach* 78 (1910): 56–66; Bronislaus Switalski, *Der Wahrheitsbegriff der Pragmatismus nach William James* (Braunsberg: Bender, 1910); J. G. Ubbink, *Het Pragmatisme van William James* (Arnhem: Tamminga, 1912).

of us knows the world in a particular way and from a particular side. In each of these resides a specific energy that corresponds to the distinct works that the objective world confers to the senses.

Thus, all intellectual knowledge begins with sense perception. To acquire knowledge, Scripture refers man not to his own reason but to God's revelation in all his works. Lift up your eyes, and see the one who has created all things; [lift them up] to the teaching and the testimony; otherwise, they shall perish. Whoever rejects the word of the Lord cannot have wisdom. This is the truth of empiricism: being is a reality to which the sense perception of the subject corresponds.

The connection between subject and object receives an even greater weight when the human being elevates himself from sense perception to science by means of thinking. Observations, provided that they are taken in the general sense and not limited to visual perception, are indeed the basis and the material of our knowledge; without them, concepts are empty, just as observations without concepts remain blind. But as the human mind [*geest*] forms concepts from representations, and from these in turn forms judgments and determinations, it already appears as if he were leaving the terra firma of reality and were building castles in the sky.

One can do away with this serious difficulty by saying that such reasoning is an altogether unpractical and useless metaphysics, but this is not an answer worthy of the man of science. The conceivability and knowability of the world is certainly the presupposition of all knowing [*weten*], but this presupposition is of such a great significance that it must be considered and ought to be justified. Whoever works scientifically must give account to himself and others of what he does and does not do. If we were inclined to neglect this objection, we would soon be rapped on the knuckles by empirical criticism. For Nietzsche is not the only one who calls the concept the "burial site of the intuition" [*begräbnisstätte einer Anschauung*];[7] Mach and Avenarius[8] are also of the opinion that when we speak of an entity [*lichaam*], only certain visual, tactile, and thermal perceptions are actually and objectively given to us. In their view, the world consists not of physical things and psychical subjects but rather of colors, tones, pressures, temperatures, spaces, times, and so on—that is, of the simplest parts of our perception. When we nevertheless speak of entities [*lichamen*], we do so only because we cannot take up each sensation separately, thus leading us, out of a practical and economic concern, to sum up a number of sensations that usually appear in connection with each other into a group. Representations and concepts do not thus correspond to an objective reality but are abbreviations, "thought symbols" [*Gedankensymbole*] for a group of

---

7. Cited in Rittelmeyer, *Friedrich Nietzsche*, 15.
8. Ernst Mach (1838–1916) was an Austrian physicist and philosopher, and Richard Avenarius (1843–1896) was a German philosopher. Both developed (though independently) forms of empirical criticism based on experience as fundamental.—Ed.

elements that usually appear in connection with each other. They have no intellectual but only psychological value; they serve as temporary aids to orient us to the world provisionally and to support us practically. It is not the entities [*lichamen*] that bring forth sensations in us, but rather, it is the groups of sensations formed by us that form the entities [*lichamen*]. And so what is posed is not only the objectivity of the world but also the subjectivity of man. The *I* is not an objectively existing reality and is nothing but a group of elements that usually appear together; it does not form something real but only an ideal, a unity produced by practical reason [*denk-oeconomische eenheid*], which changes with every passing moment.[9]

---

9. Ernst Mach, *Populärwissenschaftliche Vorlesungen*, 2nd ed. (Leipzig: Barth, 1897) [translated by Thomas J. McCormack as *Popular Scientific Lectures* (La Salle, IL: Open Court, 1986)—Ed.]; Mach, *Erkenntnis und Irrtum: Skizzen zur Psychologie der Forschung* (Leipzig: Barth, 1905) [translated by Thomas J. McCormack and Paul Foulkes as *Knowledge and Error: Sketches on the Psychology of Enquiry* (Dordrecht: D. Reidel, 1976)—Ed.]; Richard Avenarius, *Kritik der reinen Erfahrung* (Leipzig: Reisland, 1888–1890); Max Verworn, *Naturwissenschaft und Weltanschauung* (Leipzig: Barth, 1904); Verworn, *Die Mechanik des Geisteslebens* (Leipzig: Teubner, 1907). Connected to this is the immanent philosophy of Van Schuppe, Schubert-Soldern, M. R. Kaufman, et al. Cf. Richard Hönigswald, *Zur kritik der Machschen Philosophie: eine erkenntnistheoretische Studie* (Berlin: Schwetschke, 1903); Bernhard Hell, *Ernst Mach's Philosophie* (Stuttgart: Frommann, 1907); Oskar Ewald, *Richard Avenarius als Begründer des Empiriokritizismus* (Berlin: Hofmann, 1905); C. B. Spruyt, *Her empiriocriticisme, de jongste vorm van de wijsbegeerte der ervaring* (Amsterdam: De Bussy, 1899); A. Schapira, *Erkenntnistheoretische Strömungen der Gegenwart: Schuppe, Wundt und Sigwart als Erkenntnistheoretiker* (Bern: Scheitlin Spring, 1904); John Bernhard Stallo, *Die Begriffe und Theorien der modernen Physik* (Leipzig: Barth, 1901); Hans Kleinpeter, *Die Erkenntnistheorie der Naturforschung der Gegenwart* (Leipzig: Barth, 1905); Johannes Wilhelm Classen, *Vorlesungen über moderne Naturphilosophen* (Hamburg: C. Boysen, 1908); Dominicus Gerbrandus Jelgersma, "Modern Positivisme," *Gids* (October–November 1904); Bernard Hendrik Cornelis Karel van der Wijck, "Hedendaagsch Positivisme," *Onze Eeuw* (May 1905): 228–97; Willem Koster, *De Ontkenning van het bestaan der materie en de moderne physiologische psychologie* (Haarlem: Tjeenk Willink, 1904).

How the greatest uncertainty and the grossest confusion now rules over the field of the mind (*kenleer*) is clearly shown by Konstantin Kempf, "Der Bankrott der modernen Erkenntniskritik," *Stimmen aus Maria-Laach* 79 (1910): 146–56. Cf.

Now it is indeed undeniable that our representations are connections of a mass of different perceptions received by our different senses, and these concepts, in turn, are abstractions and combinations, formed out of a great number of diverse representations. There is no experimental, mathematical proof available that our representations and concepts correspond to an objective reality. Whoever desires such a proof prior to believing in an objective world of subjects and objects sets a condition that is in no way receptive to fulfillment. Even then he is also forced to deny perception all transcendent value, for here, too, there is no conclusive argument to be brought forth that the sensations are caused by an objective world of colors, sounds, movements, and so on. And also if one edges away from this skeptical consequence, the nominalistic view of representations and concepts renders all science and all truth an illusion. This is, moreover, acknowledged by Mach himself, for example. For after he first exposes the subjective character of all representations and concepts, he goes on to show that their formation is provided by the practical, economic, and teleological side of our cognitive faculty and is necessary for the acquisition of science: "All our attempts to reflect the world in our thinking would come to nothing if we were not able to find something enduring in all the kaleidoscopic change."[10] The origin and

---

Leonard Nelson, *Ueber das sogennante Erkenntnisproblem* (Göttingen: Vandenhoeck & Ruprecht, 1908).

10. Though Bavinck does not provide a citation here, he was working with the second edition of Mach's work. This quotation can be found in Mach, *Populärwis-*

application of science is "bound to the great constancy of our environment."[11] How such an enduring stability is found with Mach's view of subject and object is difficult to see. It finally comes down to the conclusion that the human person, for the sake of his economic interests, attributes to subject and object the predicate of endurance [*bestendigheid*], which they do not have in themselves. It is the human being that brings order and regularity into phenomena and thus turns them into nature. He creates the "sufficient uniformity of our environment"[12] necessary for science. The intellect is here, according to Kant himself, "the legislation for nature."[13]

In the end, then, in spite of its own testimony, empirical criticism declares that science presupposes a being, something permanent and enduring, within the fluctuating of phenomena, and thus an essence, an idea of things. And if it believes that it cannot find this in the object, it places it into the object from the subject, allowing nature to be formed by the human being.

However, this is no more than a desperate move [*noodsprong*]. For it is one or the other: the human intellect does this wholly arbitrarily, without the objective

senschaftliche Vorlesungen, 216. Bavinck gives the quotation in German, "Alle unsere Bemühungen, die Welt in Gedanken abzuspiegeln, wären fruchtlos, wenn es nicht gelänge, in dem bunten Wechsel Bleibendes zu finde."—Ed.

11. Mach, *Populärwissenschaftliche Vorlesungen*, 223. Bavinck gives the quotation in German: "Eine grosse Beständigkeit unserer Umgebung gebunden."—Ed.

12. Bavinck gives the quotation in German: "hinreichende Gleichförmigkeit unserer Umgebung."—Ed.

13. Cited in Hönigswald, *Ueber die Lehre Humes von der Realität der Aussendinge*, 27. [Bavinck gives the quotation in German: "die Gesetzgebung für die Natur."—Ed.]

world offering any grounds for it, which means that the phenomenal world is shaped by our mind, nothing but an image of a dream, and thus, according to Nietzsche's view, is simply something that we make up. Or the intellect is justified in doing this; it acts in accordance with its endowed nature and being, presupposing, too, that nature itself, which is interpreted by the intellect, contains the information for it. And as such, the intellect and nature must both exist in thought—the former subjectively and the latter objectively—and be brought forth from it.

"For all knowledge," says rightly Berlin professor Ferdinand Jakob Schmidt,[14] "that expresses not merely subjective, empirical certainty but objective truth is grounded on the categories, axioms, and ideas that originate from the general unity of spirit in universal existence and life. And without this, there is no scientific knowledge, to whichever specific area it might pertain."[15] And H. Rickert, in his book *The Limits of Concept Formation in Natural Science*,[16] demonstrates most emphatically the reasons why the world-governing [*wereldbeheerschende*]

---

14. Ferdinand Jakob Schmidt (1860–1939) was a German philosopher.—Ed.

15. Ferdinand Jakob Schmidt, *Der Niedergang der Protestantismus* (Berlin: Weidmann, 1904), 4. [Bavinck gives the quotation in German: "Denn alles Wissen das nicht bloss subjective, empirische Gewissheit sondern objective Wahrheit ausdrückt, ist gegründet auf die aus der allgemeinen Geisteseinheit des universellen Daseins und Lebens entspringende Kategorien, Grundsätze und Ideen, und ohne diese gibt es këine wissenschaftlichte Erkenntnis, auf welches Sondergebiet sie auch immer gerichtet sein mag."—Ed.]

16. Heinrich Rickert (1863–1936) was a German neo-Kantian philosopher. See Rickert, *Die Grenzen der naturwissenschaftlichen Begriffsbildung: Eine Logische Einleitung in die historischen Wissenschaften*, 6th ed. (Tübingen: Mohr Siebeck, 1929). Translated by Guy Oakes as *The Limits of Concept Formation in Natural Science: A Logical Introduction to the Historical Sciences* (Cambridge: Cambridge University Press, 1986).—Ed.]

goodwill is the presupposition behind all our thinking and knowing.[17] No matter how we look at it, the concept of truth and science—if we think consistently and without prejudice—brings us to Christian theism.

This teaches us that all things are brought forth from the wisdom of the Word of God and thus, in Augustine's words, that all things exist according to "reason" [*rationes*], in measure, number, and weight. Scripture understands this not in a pantheistic sense, according to which all things would have originated from a contentless "reason" [*Vernunft*], an unconscious identical with a "superconscious" [*Überbewusste*], an illogical will, or a blind force of nature. For how would the ideas, which are in the world, ever be able to find an explanation of their origin there? Just as materialism is capable of understanding thinking [*het denken*] as a product of material alterations [*stof-wisseling*], so it is possible for atheism to explain the world out of the unconscious, calling this either reason or will. If the world can be the content of our knowing, it must itself be clear and distinguished by thought beforehand. Only as all things are from the "foreknowledge" [προγνωσις] of God are they altogether a "manifestation" [φανερωσις] of his thoughts. The *universalia* are *in re*, for they existed *ante rem* in the divine consciousness [*bewustzijn*]. The world would not be known to us if it did not exist, but it would not exist

---

17. Cf. Heinrich Rickert, *Der Gegenstand des Erkenntnis: Einführung in die Transzendental-philosophie*, 2nd ed. (Tübingen: Mohr Siebeck, 1904).

if it were not thought of beforehand by God. We know the things because they are, but they are because God has known them.[18] The doctrine of the creation of all things by the Word of God is the explanation of all knowing and knowing about [*kennen en weten*], the presupposition behind the correspondence between subject and object. Just as the senses concur with the elements of things, so does the understanding respond to thought, which binds the elements to things, to bodies, to a nature and the world. For "what is seen" [το βλεπομενον] did not come to be "out of the visible" [εχ φαινομενων] (Heb. 11:3); the "invisible attributes of God" [ἀορατα του θεου] can be "perceived" [νοουμενα] through his works, becoming beheld by the "mind" [νους] (Rom. 1:18).[19] The *universalia in re* move over into our consciousness along the path of sense perception, then through the thinking activity of the "mind" [νους]. The world becomes, and can only become, our spiritual [*geestelijk*] property, for it is itself existing spiritually [*geestelijk*] and logically and resting in thought.

Hence, we now gain this great and rich advantage—that for us, objective truth is displayed to us in all the works of God's hands, in nature and history, in creation and re-creation. The knowable [*weetbare*] precedes our science [*wetenschap*], just as the faith that we believe pre-

---

18. Augustine, *Conf.* 13.38; *Civ.* 9.10.
19. Though Bavinck cites Rom. 1:18 here, he is paraphrasing more directly the wording of Rom. 1:20.—Ed.

cedes the faith by which we believe. The objects of knowledge are the measure of knowledge.[20] And the deeper one thinks this through, [the clearer it becomes that] all truth is understood in the Wisdom, in the Word, who was in the beginning with God and who himself was God. The one who denies this Wisdom undermines the "foundation" [*fundamentum*] of all science, for "whoever denies ideas, denies the Son" [*qui negat ideas, negat Filium*].[21] On this Christian standpoint, all autonomy of the human mind falls away, as if it could produce truth out of its own reason and through its own means. The human being is not the creator and former of the world; his understanding does not write its laws on nature, and in his scientific research he does not have to arrange things according to his categories. To the contrary, it is the human who has to conform his perception and thinking to God's revelation in nature and grace: "Reality does not have to make itself comply with our reason, but rather, on the basis of the whole experience of the whole age, our thinking must seek to lay bare the metaphysic that God has woven into reality."[22] To enter into the realm of truth, we must

---

20. Otto Willmann, *Geschichte des Idealismus* (Braunschweig: F. Vieweg und Sohn, 1896), 2:403. [The latter part of this line is composed of Latin phrases: ". . . zooals de *fides, quae* aan de *fides, qua creditor. Scibilia sunt mensural scientiae.*" Furthermore, though Bavinck does not cite the specific edition of Willman's work from which he is drawing, it is likely that he was working with the 1896 edition, since the first edition of *Christian Worldview* was published in 1904, which preceded the 1907 edition of *Geschichte des Idealismus.*—Ed.]

21. Willmann, *Geschichte des Idealismus*, 3:802.

22. Gustav Portig, *Das Weltgesetz des kleinsten Kraftaufwandes in den Reichen der Natur*, vol. 1, *In der Mathematik, Physik und Chemie* (Stuttgart: Kielmann, 1903), cited in *Beweis des Glaubens* (September–October 1904): 260. [Bavinck gives the quotation in German: "Nicht hat sich die Wirklichkeit nach unserer Vernunft zu

become children: "It is of nature to bring forth, and freedom, the freedom brought from truth."[23] All knowledge
consists in the conformity of our consciousness to the
objective truth. One thus knows the truth to the extent
that he himself is in the truth. To understand the truth,
one must be of the truth.[24]

But even with sense perception and science, with representations and concepts, the human mind does not
stand still. It is not satisfied with these but strives above
both toward a comprehensive wisdom.[25] Science and
wisdom are doubtless closely related, but they are not
identical. In former times, Aristotle's distinction was nor-
mally granted, that science [*wetenschap*] consisted in "the
knowledge of the thing through the *proximate cause*,"[26]
while wisdom, on the other hand, stretched toward "the
knowledge of the thing through the *primary cause*."[27]
This distinction has remained in force up to the present
day. It is true, however, that in the last century, out of a
reaction against the aprioristic speculation of Hegel and

---

richten, sondern unser Denken muss auf Grund der Gesamterfahrung eines ganzen
Weltalters die von Gott in die Wirklichkeit verwobene Metaphysiek blosszulegen
suchen."—Ed.]

23. Bavinck gives the quotation in Latin: "Naturae parere, libertas, libertas ex
veritate." Bavinck deploys these same terms and this same pattern of reasoning in his
"Evolution," in *Essays on Religion, Science, and Society*, ed. John Bolt, trans. Harry
Boonstra and Gerrit Sheeres (Grand Rapids, MI: Baker Academic, 2008), 113.—Ed.

24. Willmann, *Geschichte des Idealismus*, 2:993.

25. According to Cicero's account, the name *sophoi* ["wise men"], which was
first used by the Greeks, was turned into *philosophoi* ["philosophers"] by Pythago-
ras, on the grounds that wisdom pertains to God alone, whereas humans can only
desire and strive for wisdom.

26. Bavinck gives the quotation in Latin: "cognitio rei per causam *proximam*"
(italics original).—Ed.

27. Bavinck gives the quotation in Latin: "cognitio rei per causam *primam*"
(italics original).—Ed.

his school, the wisdom of the heritage of knowledge was banished, and the right of existence for all metaphysics was denied. Science had to limit itself in a positivist sense to the investigation of the phenomena and of their mutual connections, the *nexus rerum*.[28] And as long as science itself lived in the delusion, and gave others the illusion, that it would solve all the riddles of the world and life, it could, in naïve innocence, deem all philosophy superfluous. But when the mysteries increased from all sides in advanced research, wisdom itself had to assert its rights again and claim a place in the field of human knowledge. Metaphysics, philosophy, world-and-life view currently celebrate their glorious return, not only in theology and the humanities [*geesteswetenschappen*][29] but also in the natural sciences [*wetenschap der natuur*].[30] The human mind does not set a limit for itself in its search for knowledge, not even with Kant or Comte.[31] If science [*wetenschap*] does not quench its thirst for truth, it eagerly stretches out toward the source of wisdom. After all, humanity has not only the faculty of perception [*waarnemingsvermogen*]

28. This Latin term denotes the universal connections that bind all things together.—Ed.

29. G. Wobbermin, *Theologie und Metaphysik: Das Verhältnis der Theologie zur Modernen Erkenntnistheorie und Psychologie* (Berlin: Duncker, 1901); Johannes Wendland, "Philosophie und Religion," *Theologische Studien und Kritiken* (1903): 517–85; Emil Pfennigsdorf, "Theologie und Metaphysik," *Theologische Rundschau* (1904): 399–413; Herman Groenewegen, *De Theologie en hare wijsbegeerte* (Amsterdam: Rogge, 1904).

30. Wilhelm Ostwald, *Vorlesungen über Naturphilosophie* (Leipzig: Veit, 1902); Ostwald, *Grundriss der Naturphilosophie* (Leipzig: Reclam, 1908); Reinke, *De Welt als That*; Hans Driesch, *Naturbegriffe und Natururteile* (Leipzig: Engelmann, 1904); Alfred Dippe, *Naturphilosophie: Kritische Einführung in die modernen Lehren über Kosmos und Menschheit* (München: Beck, 1907).

31. Auguste Comte (1798–1857) was a French philosopher.—Ed.

and a mind [*verstand*] but also reason, which can find rest and satisfaction only in the "Absolute" [*Unbedingte*].

The distinction between wisdom and science does not, however, sever its connection with this truth. True wisdom is not served by aprioristic speculation; it has not to do with tenuous theories but with knowledge of reality. Just as sense perception is the basis [*grondslag*] of all science, the results of science are and remain the starting point of philosophy. Yet it is incorrect that philosophy should be no more than the summary of the results of the various sciences and that they should be set together only as the wheels of a clock.[32] Wisdom is grounded on science but is not limited to it. It aims above science and seeks to press through to "first principles" [*prima principia*]. It already does this if it makes a special group of phenomena—religion, ethics, law, history, language, culture, and so on—into the object of its reflection [*denkende beschouwing*] and tries to trace the leading ideas therein. But it does this, above all, as it seeks for the final grounds of all things and builds a worldview thereon.

If this is the nature and task of philosophy, then it is presupposed—to an even greater degree than sense perception and science—that the world rests in thought and that ideas control all things. There is no wisdom other than that which is in and out of the faith in a realm of unseen and eternal things. It is built on the reality of ideas,

---

32. Tilmann Pesch, *Die grossen Welträthsel*, 2nd ed. (Freiburg: Herder, 1892), 1:69.

because it is indeed the "science of the idea" [*Wissenschaft der Idee*] and because it seeks the idea of the whole in the parts and of the general in the particular.[33] It tacitly proceeds from the Christian faith, which states that the world is grounded in wisdom and reveals wisdom in its whole and in all its parts (Ps. 104:24; Prov. 3:19; 1 Cor. 1:21). It is the same divine wisdom [*Goddelijke wijsheid*] that created the world organically into a connected whole and planted in us the urge for a "unified" [*einheitliche*] worldview. If this is possible, it can be explained only on the basis of the claim that the world is an organism and has first been thought of as such. Only then do philosophy and worldview have a right and ground of existence, as it is also on this high point of knowledge that subject and object harmonize, as the reason within us corresponds with the *principia* of all being and knowing. And what philosophy has demanded according to its essence is then guaranteed and explained for us by the testimony of God in his word. It is the same divine wisdom that gives things existence and our thought objective validity, that bestows intelligibility to things and the power of thinking [*denkkracht*] to our mind, that makes the things *real* and our thoughts [*denkbeelden*] *true*. The intelligibility of things is the content of our intellect. Both being and knowing [*het zijn en het kennen*] have their "reason" [*ratio*] in the Word, through whom God created all things.[34]

---

33. Trendelenburg, *Logische Untersuchungen*, 1:5, 6; 2:461.
34. Willmann, *Geschichte des Idealismus*, 1:279, 433 cf. 541, etc.

Finally, it is from this high and glorious standpoint, on which Christian wisdom places us, that a surprising light is cast on the relationship of religion and philosophy. All great thinkers have felt and recognized their kinship. Led by his dialectical method, Hegel came to the view that religion was the primitive philosophy, the allegory-shrouded, imaginative metaphysics [*aanschouwelijke metaphysica*] of the common people [*volk*], and thus that philosophy is religion transposed into concepts by thinkers. In so doing, he fell short in describing the essence of both, particularly so in the case of religion. For even if it were true that philosophy could provide a complete explanation of the world and a perfectly pure concept of God, it would still not be enough for the human being. The thirst of his heart goes forth not primarily for a pure concept of God [*Godsbegrip*] but for the living God himself. The human being finds no rest until God becomes *his* God and *his* Father. While philosophy may have such a glorious task and calling, we ourselves do not find God [when led] by her hand; we approach him, we enter into fellowship with him, only by way of religion. Even for the deepest thinker, there is no justification thanks to the concept [of Hegel];[35] it is only from faith. Jesus, God be thanked, pronounced not the wise and the prudent blessed but rather the little ones, those who are small among the philosophers. Bet-

---

35. Just as Dr. G. A. van den Bergh van Eysinga claims, in *Allegorische Interpretatie* (Amsterdam: P. N. van Kampen & Zoon, 1904), 28. [Here Bavinck refers to Gustaaf Adolf van den Bergh van Eysinga (1874–1957), a Dutch New Testament scholar who belonged to the Dutch school of Radical Criticism.—Ed.]

ter than Hegel's method was the idea of Schleiermacher,[36] who derived religion and philosophy from two totally distinct needs and functions of human nature and thus ensured an enduring place for both in human life. But this dualism also does not satisfy: philosophy is not limited to the finite, and thus it also comes in contact with God as the final cause of all things; and religion, bringing the human being first into fellowship with God, thereby also determines his relationship to all creatures. It does not proceed in passionate feelings [*gevoelsaandoeningen*] but follows very concrete representations [*voorstellingen*] and always contains in seed form a whole worldview.[37]

Now by the nature of things, a worldview is always "unified" [*einheitlich*]. As long as we have not understood, however, all the realms and spheres of creation as parts of a whole, our worldview is not rounded out and complete. Of course, the question here is not whether we have already brought our worldview to that point or ever shall do so, but the concept implies harmonious unity. As such, there can be no essentially different worldview in religion and in philosophy, for the common people and for the learned, for the academy and for life. If religion contains a worldview in seed form, and philosophy, in searching for the final ground of all things, always seeks

---

36. Friedrich Schleiermacher (1768–1834) was a German theologian influential in the rise of modern Protestant theology.—Ed.

37. On the distinction between philosophy and worldview, see Hans Richert, *Philosophie: Ihr Wesen, ihre Probleme, ihre Literatur* (Leipzig: Teubner, 1912), 18; on that between world imagery [*wereldbeeld*] and worldview [*wereldbeschouwing*], see C. Wenzig, *Die Weltanschauungen der Gegenwart* (Leipzig: Quelle and Meyer, 1907), 1.

after God, then it follows naturally that they, in all their distinctions, have to conform inwardly to the essence of the matter and cannot compete with each other.

Only the Christian worldview can fulfill this demand, because it makes known to us one God, the living and true God, and cuts the root of all polytheism. There is not a different God for the child and the elderly person, for the simple and the learned, for the heart and the head. The separation, an imitation of Gnosticism now made by many between exoteric and esoteric doctrine, between representation and concept, between fact and idea, is in principle unacceptable. In pedagogical terms, it gives rise to all sorts of misunderstanding and untruthful conduct. In addition to this, it fails to recognize both the ideal reality of being and the tethering of consciousness to the world of reality. It is incorrect to claim that truth can be found only *in* and *for* the concept [*het begrip*] and that everything else is image and likeness.[38] For we do not have enough in blind facts and empty ideas. Hence, in the Christian religion both are intimately united. Creation and re-creation are acts of God in time, but at the same time, they are the embodiment of his eternal counsel. The philosophy that remains true to its own idea and does not lose itself in vain speculation thus leads to the same God revealed to us by the Christian religion as a God of wisdom and grace. And the Christian religion makes

---

38. Van den Bergh van Eysinga, *Allegorische Interpretatie*, 28.

known to us that same theism by its revelation, which upon unprejudiced investigation is made known to be the basis of all science [*wetenschap*] and philosophy. The same God needed by the pious believer and the philosopher is the one who makes himself known to both in his works. It is the same Word who made all things and who, in the fullness of time, became flesh. The same Spirit who renews the face of the earth changes the heart of the sinner. And thus: *verus philosophus amator Dei* ["The true philosopher is a lover of God"], and: *Christianus verus philosophus* ["A Christian is a true philosopher"].[39]

---

39. Cf. Lactantius, who, in the fourth book of his *Divinae Institutiones*, provides a discourse on "true wisdom" [*vera sapientia*] and "religion" [*religione*] and therein shows the indissoluble relationship between the two. [An English translation is available as Lactantius, *The Divine Institutes, Books I–VII*, vol. 49 of *The Fathers of the Church*, trans. Mary Francis McDonald (Washington, DC: Catholic University of America Press, 1964).—Ed.]

2

Being and Becoming

The second problem solved in our worldview is that of being and becoming, of unity and multiplicity, of God and world. And for this, Christianity is also of fundamental significance.

At first appearance, the world appears to us as a chaotic multiplicity of phenomena, as an endless number of things that constantly come and go like waves on the ocean. But if we let ourselves be led by our spirit's urge for unity and look more deeply into the phenomena, we discover a harmony and fitness for purpose in the multiplicity, which brings us to the conviction that the world cannot be the product of an independent, accidental confluence of elements. From antiquity, two philosophical directions stood in opposition to each other. According to one, there was only being and no becoming. Change and movement were a facade; time and space were but subjective "ways of thinking" [*modi cogitandi*]. The concept of becoming was regarded as even containing an antinomy, because a thing had to stay itself while simultaneously transferring into something else. And according to the other direction, being was nothing more than an "object of thought" [*Gedankendig*]; only becoming was real. Everything but invariability was variable, but this, like the identity of being and nothingness, was necessary and pertained to the absolute self; it lay in the nature of absolute becoming, to contradict itself and through constant contradiction with itself to come to its full development.

Between these one-sided directions, other thinkers have looked for a "mediation" [*Vermittelung*], a reconciliation. In this manner, atomism tries to explain the world from a mechanism of immutable, material, soulless atoms. The fruit of philosophical rumination rather than exact science, this approach had already emerged in antiquity and was praised, especially since the middle of the previous century, as the solution to all the world's problems. Diverse causes—such as the reaction to speculative philosophy, the blossoming of the natural sciences and material welfare—have enabled it to master the spirit for a considerable time. Without these, it would be hard to understand how such a worldview could gain acceptance among intelligent people. The effective objection against it, that accidentally throwing thousands of letters together never produces a single *Iliad*, still stands.[1]

Recent years have seen some change in this regard. At first, a lone voice dared timidly suggest that life and consciousness, freedom and efficiency could not be explained from the mechanical circulation of matter. One had to be brave to say this, because whoever dared to do so paid—in some circles—with his reputation as a scientist. The "seven world riddles" [*Sieben Welträthsel*] of du Bois-Reymond[2] were, according to Haeckel, proof of his advancing old age and of his weakened mental capacity.[3] And the reception that was recently given to Professor Reinke of Kiel[4] at the philosophical congress in Geneva, with his subject "Neovitalism and the meaning of teleology in biology," led to the question whether philosophers can be biased.[5] Slowly, however, the number of those who consider the mechanical explanation of phenomena to be wholly inadequate has increased. There is a sense in which Oscar Hertwig[6] witnessed in their name

---

1. Bavinck is alluding to the ancient Greek epic poem commonly attributed to Homer.—Ed.

2. Emil du Bois-Reymond (1818–1896) was a German physician and physiologist. Du Bois-Reymond argued for the existence of seven "world riddles" that lay beyond the explanative powers of both science and philosophy: (1) the ultimate nature of matter and force, (2) the origin of motion, (3) the origin of life, (4) the "apparently teleological arrangements of nature," (5) the origin of simple sensations, (6) the origin of intelligent thought and language, and (7) the question of free will. Gabriel Ward Finkelstein, *Emil du Bois-Reymond: Neuroscience, Self, and Society in Nineteenth-Century Germany* (Cambridge, MA: MIT Press, 2013), 272–73.—Ed.

3. Ernst Haeckel, *Die Welträthsel* (Bonn: E. Strauss, 1899), 118.

4. Johannes Reinke (1849–1931) was a German botanist and philosopher.—Ed.

5. *Handelsblad*, September 16, 1904.

6. Oscar Hertwig (1849–1922) was a German zoologist.—Ed.

for some years "that the explanation of the world as a mechanism of colliding atoms is based on a fiction, which may be useful for some conditions but which does not correspond to reality itself."[7]

Objection to this argument has come primarily from biology. The problem of life remained and was not simply bulldozed by mechanical monism. To the extent that it was researched more deeply, it seemed all the more to be a mystery. Haeckel could maintain his old standpoint and call neovitalism[8] a "fruitful cerebral epidemic," regarding which he could only comfort himself with the hope that it would pass quickly.[9] Nonetheless, he had to look on as many biologists, including even some of his own students, returned to the previously disdained concept of life force. Pasteur[10] demonstrated that the rule "all life is from life" [*omne vivum ex vivo*] also held true for microbes. The investigations of Mohl and Nägeli, of Remak, Kölliker, and Virchow[11] showed that the multiplication of cells happened only through reproduction and thus took place

---

7. Oscar Hertwig, *Die Entwicklung der Biologie im 19. Jahrhundert* (Jena: Fischer, 1900), 30. [Bavinck gives the quotation in German: "Dass die Erklärung der Welt als eines Mechanismus sich stossender Atome nur auf einer Fiktion beruht, welche zur Darstellung mancher Verhältnisse nützlich sein mag, aber doch nicht der Wirklichkeit selbst entspricht."—Ed.]

8. Neovitalism was a nineteenth-century movement that rejected strict materialism, claiming instead that the most essential properties of life could not be grasped by the natural sciences.—Ed.

9. Haeckel, *Die Welträthsel*, 444.

10. Louis Pasteur (1822–1895) was a French biologist and chemist.—Ed.

11. Bavinck is referring to Hugo von Mohl (1805–1872), the German botanist; Carl Nägeli (1817–1891), the Swiss botanist; Robert Remak (1815–1865), the Polish-German embryologist, neurologist, and physiologist; Albert von Kölliker (1817–1905), the Swiss anatomist, physiologist, and histologist; and Rudolf Virchow (1821–1902), the Swiss pathologist.—Ed.

according to a rule: "all cells come from cells" [*omnis cellula e cellula*]. Despite all the progress of science, as Hertwig rightly said, the rift between the lifeless and the living nature of life, rather than being filled, only became broader and deeper. The machine theory of life seemed to be false. Powers other than the chemical and physical were at work in the world.[12]

As a consequence to this reaction in the realm of biology, many have exchanged the materialistic-mechanical worldview for the dynamic, or the energetic. The natural sciences always have to deal with four fundamental concepts: space, time, substance, and energy.[13] Regarding the first two, there is no difference of meaning, as all must accept these forms of existence alongside and after each other. But this is different with the two other concepts of substance and energy (quantity and causality; matter and energy). While materialism regards matter as an eternal substance and energy as pertaining to it, dynamism, to the contrary, sees energy as original

---

12. Hertwig, *Die Entwicklung der Biologie*, 9, 24. See also Johannes Reinke, *Die Welt als That* (Berlin: Paetel, 1903), 155; Hans Driesch, *Naturbegriffe und Natururteile* (Leipzig: Engelmann, 1904), 97–127; Eduard von Hartmann, "Mechanismus und Vitalismus in der modernen Biologie," *Archiv für systematische Philosophie* (1903): 139–74, 331–76; Rudolf Otto, "Darwinismus von heute und Theologie," *Theologische Rundschau* 7, no. 2 (1904): 540; Otto, "Die mechanistische Lebenstheorie und die Theologie," *Zeitschrift für Theologie und Kirche* 13, no. 3 (1903): 179–213; Otto, "Die Ueberwindung der mechanistischen Lehre vom Leben in der heutigen Naturwissenschaft," *Zeitschrift für Theologie und Kirche* 14, no. 3 (1904): 234–72; R. P. Mees, *De mechanische verklaring der levensverschijnselen* ('s-Gravenhage: Martinus Nijhoff, 1899); L. Bouman, "Over theoretische Biologie," in *Orgaan van de Christelijke Vereeniging voor Natuur- en Geneeskundigen in Nederland* (1904): 43–67.

13. Eduard von Hartmann, *Die Weltanschauung der modernen Physik* (Leipzig: Haacke, 1902), 186; Driesch, *Naturbegriffe und Natururteile*, 38.

and material as derivative. According to this theory, the primordial elements of things are immaterial and punctual, that is, being found at defined points in space and with centers of power, or dynamides,[14] equipped with definite energies. To be able to explain the phenomenon of matter, however, a materializing [*materiirende*] power is assumed, which calls to the fore the appearance of a material filling of space.[15]

Although this dynamic worldview is to be valued insofar as it sheds light on the insufficiency of materialism, it must certainly face up to no less serious objections. It immediately seems impossible to form a clear concept or representation of these primordial elements of things. If they are indeed what they are called, they cannot be thought of as other than mathematical points or as existing in the manner of ghosts or souls, which is as "simple beings" [*entia simplicia*], with a "definitive existence" [*existentia definitiva*]. Such "beings" [*entia*], however, may not, and cannot, be real, because they exist only in centers of power, or dynamides. But how, in that case, is a real, objective existence granted? Should one wish to assert the objective reality of dynamides against this, there exists no other possibility than that one views them as operations of the single, absolute

---

14. Here Bavinck refers to the work of Philipp Lenard (1862–1947), the Austrian physicist who advanced the idea that the atom was an assemblage of "dynamides."—Ed.

15. Von Hartmann, *Die Weltanschauung der modernen Physik*, 183; Otto Liebmann, *Gedanken und Thatsachen* (Strasbourg: Trübner, 1901), 2:128–32.

being. The dynamism of Eduard von Hartmann[16] comes forth in this form. He recognizes that "activity without an active element" [*Thätigkeit ohne ein Thätiges*] cannot exist and that, accordingly, powers make the appearance of matter and finite bodies possible. He concludes, therefore, that the atoms in the absolute substance regain that substance, which is as such denied to them: "With regard to the absolute substance, they cease to be activities without an action; i.e., ontologically, they hang in the air."[17] On the basis of this change in the view of nature, the philosophy of the unconscious has also not neglected to make advances in its monistic philosophy. This change, though, seems to many to consist in little more than a move from materialism to pantheism, from atomism to dynamism—a change that even Haeckel (to an extent) seems to perceive when he calls atoms, together with energy and matter, with the incorporeal and the material elements, "living."[18] Hylozoism[19] and panpsychism[20] come close to each other, as the former ascends to the mental image of "conscious

16. Eduard von Hartmann (1842–1906) was a German metaphysical philosopher.—Ed.

17. Von Hartmann, *Die Weltanschauung der modernen Physik*, 204–9; von Hartmann, *Philosophie des Unbewussten* (Leipzig: Haacke, 1904), 2:495. [An English translation is available as Eduard von Hartmann, *Philosophy of the Unconscious: Speculative Results according to the Inductive Method of Physical Science*, trans. William Coupland, 9th ed. (London: Routledge, 2000).—Ed.]

18. Ernst Haeckel, *Der Monismus als Band zwischen Religion und Wissenschaft* (Bonn: Strauss, 1893), 14, 17, 33.

19. Hylozoism refers to the view that matter itself is in some sense alive. It was prominent in ancient Greek philosophy and saw a revival of interest in both the Renaissance and early modern periods.—Ed.

20. Panpsychism refers to a spectrum of views broadly sharing the belief that the cosmos itself possesses a mind, consciousness, or soul.—Ed.

matter," whereas the latter descends to the idea of "unconscious spirit."[21]

Whenever one is not satisfied, however, with the empiriocriticism[22] of such speculation and wants to remove the absolute and the transcendent from science entirely, it goes without saying that dynamides also bear far too metaphysical a character. Atoms and dynamides are imperceptible and depend entirely on the Platonic method of actualizing concepts and thus granting them a reality beyond consciousness; therefore, one must break with this method. We must keep to what is positively given and may not go behind it. These givens are, according to Mach, Ostwald,[23] Helm,[24] et al., only energies and effects. All that we know of the external world we can express "in the form of statements about existing energies" [*in der Gestalt von Aussagen über vorhandene Energieën*]. Our science can bring us no further. Energies are the final details, the real facts, to which we have recourse and from which we must thus always proceed. Matter and spirit, subject and object, the physical and the psychic, substances and "things in themselves" [*Dingen an sich*] have no objective existence. They are nothing more than a group of diverse energies summarized by our reason.[25]

---

21. Von Hartmann, *Philosophie des Unbewussten*, 3:vii.

22. Empiriocriticism is the notion that philosophy is tasked with the formulation of a natural view of the world based on pure experience.—Ed.

23. Wilhelm Ostwald (1853–1932) was a Russian-German chemist and philosopher and the recipient of the 1909 Nobel Prize for chemistry.—Ed.

24. Georg Helm (1851–1923) was a German mathematician.—Ed.

25. Richard Hönigswald, *Zur kritik der Machschen Philosophie: eine erkenntnistheoretische Studie* (Berlin: Schwetschke, 1903); Rudolf Eisler, *Wörterbuch der*

As with atomism, this energetic view is also subject to critique. If one should maintain that the energies are objectively real, one becomes guilty (on that basis) of a gross inconsistency. If the transcendent and the metaphysical must be entirely banished, it is then quite illegitimate to speak of the objective reality of the energies. The only truly certain things are the perceptions of tone and color, of push and pull, of movement and change. Whoever affirms objective energies on that basis abandons positive fact and moves over to the standpoint of transcendental realism. Should the legitimacy of this conclusion—that the diverse perceptions be regarded as objectively existing—be defended, it is then the case that moving from the energies to their substances and carriers may be denied on the basis of this rule: energy without substance is unthinkable, an effect cannot be without something that works on it, and a movement cannot be without something that moves it. No real nature can be constructed from purely formal, ideal relations.

A still more serious consideration, however, should be raised against both dynamism and energeticism. Even if the essence of matter is unknown to us, we nonetheless all have experience, through consciousness, of a series of properties that could be caused only by a material substance. How could impermeability, mass, inertia, expansion, and visibility ever be derived from or made

philosophischen Begriffe, 2nd ed. (Berlin: Ernst Siegfried Mittler und Sohn, 1904), entries "Energie," "Materie."

explicable by dynamides or energies? Should we find ourselves unable to affirm a material substance on the basis of these properties and have to regard matter as a mirage and an illusion, not only do these properties remain unexplained, but also all the certainty of our knowledge is taken away. Things in themselves must then be something wholly other than whatever our capacities, in their most focused perception, make us think. Their occurrence to our perceptions is utterly different from what they really are. Our sensory organs lose their reliability, our sensory knowledge is done away with, and the conclusion that moves from appearance to essence is shipwrecked. We arrive at illusionism and subject all science to skepticism.[26]

As such, the world cannot be traced back to dynamides (or energies). Combined, the fundamental concepts of matter and energy are inadequate. This is much more the case when they are handled individually in providing us with an explanation of the inexhaustible richness of appearances that occur to us in nature. Even Plato, who undervalued the sensory world, and Aristotle, who undervalued the ideal world, were not able to avoid being entirely one-sided on this point. The full truth is first presented to us in Scripture, when it teaches that things have come forth from God's "manifold wisdom" [πολυποικιλος σοφια], that they are mutually distinguished by a

---

26. Against energism, see von Hartmann, *Die Weltanschauung der modernen Physik*, 190–99; von Hartmann, *Philosophie des Unbewussten* 2:488; Johannes Reinke, *Das energetische Weltbild* (Berlin: Deutsche Rundschau, 1908), 358; Reinke, *Die Welt als That*, 142.

common character and name, that in their multiplicity they are one, and that in their unity they are still distinct.

Nature, as regarded in the Christian religion, is thus much more capacious and richer than the concept that dominates current-day natural science. In former days this was generally the case. *Nature* encompassed the entirety of the creation, the spiritual as well as the material. Sometimes the concept was expanded even further and also applied to the Creator. God was the *natura naturans* ["the self-causing activity of nature"], the *natura summa* ["the sum of nature"], and all being, the invisible as well as the visible, the creating as well as the created, was summarized together under the one name of *nature*. But also when the concept was limited to the creature, as was regularly the case, one absolutely did not think only of the material but just as much of the spiritual creations. There was both a *natura spiritualis* ["spiritual nature"] and a *natura corporalis* ["corporeal nature"], and thus not only a *physica corporis* ["physics of the body"] but also a *physica animae* ["physics of the soul"]. *Physica* ["physics"] was usually limited to the *scientia corporis naturalis* ["the knowledge of corporeal nature"], but it was accompanied by *pneumatica*, which dealt with the doctrine of God, of angels, and of the soul.[27] But slowly nature and *physica* have acquired a far narrower meaning; nature now usually refers only to

---

27. Johann Heinrich Alsted, *Encyclopaedia septem tomis distincta* (Herbonae Nassoviorum: Corvinus Erben, 1630), 1:631, 668.

"the perceptible external and that which is set in opposition to the spirit," and *physica* has become the science of molecular movements, the doctrine of the laws that obligingly appear in lifeless nature.[28]

Based on this limited view of nature, the mechanical explanation for phenomena has every right to exist; there is no one who considers challenging it. But it is one-sided to make this small aspect of nature equal to nature itself in its entirety and to apply the method that is used here to all other phenomena. However, this has nonetheless been done by the advocates of the atomistic-mechanical worldview. Haeckel sums up monism in this sense, that there is only one "structure of the world" [*Weltgesetzlichkeit*], namely, that of causal mechanism, in the process labeling all other theories simplistically dualistic, transcendent, and supernaturalistic.[29] When du Bois-Reymond considers life and consciousness to be inexplicable on the basis of the circulation of matter, he [according to Haeckel] offers a program of metaphysical dualism.[30] When Wundt[31] maintains that psychology is a distinct area of the humanities, he has swapped [Haeckel argues] the monistic, materialistic standpoint for dualism and spiritualism.[32]

---

28. Eisler, *Wörterbuch der philosophischen Begriffe*, entries "Natur," "Physik."
29. Cf. Herman Bavinck, "Christianity and Natural Science," in *Essays on Religion, Science, and Society*, ed. John Bolt, trans. Harry Boonstra and Gerrit Sheeres (Grand Rapids, MI: Baker, 2008), 101.—Ed.
30. Haeckel, *Die Welträthsel*, 209.
31. Wilhelm Wundt (1832–1920) was a German physician, physiologist, and philosopher who is generally credited with the founding of modern experimental psychology.—Ed.
32. Haeckel, *Die Welträthsel*, 117–19. [Bavinck's original citation—"117, 109"—appears to be a typographical error.—Ed.]

The view of the soul as an independent, immaterial being is dualistic and supernaturalistic: "It asserts the existence of energies that exist without material basis and are effective; it is based on the assumption that beyond and above nature a spiritual world nonetheless exists, an immaterial world of which we know nothing by experience and of which our nature can know nothing."[33] In this, nature is simply identified with the world of physical phenomena, and the mechanical explanation [of the world] is exalted as the only scientific explanation; whatever goes beyond it is supernatural, a miracle, and miracles are naturally impossible!

However one-sided and narrow-minded this view of nature and science is, it continues to captivate many hearts.[34] Those who have abandoned the mechanical worldview as untenable continue to honor it secretly as the scientific ideal. They must necessarily admit that in one area or another, the mechanical explanation is insufficient and must be replaced or filled in by a teleological account. In this way, Reinke recognizes that "final causes" [*causa finalis*] also work alongside "primary" [*causale*] causes, although he accepts only "causal effects" [*Kausalwirkungen*] for inorganic nature.[35] And elsewhere

---

33. Haeckel, *Die Welträthsel*, 105. [Bavinck gives the quotation in German: "Denn sie behauptet die Existenz von Kräften, welche ohne materielle Basis existiren und wirksam sind; sie fusst auf der Annahme, dass ausser und über der Natur noch eine geistige Welt existire, eine immaterielle Welt, von der wir durch Erfahrung nichts wissen und unserer Natur nach nichts wissen können."—Ed.]

34. Ludwig Busse, *Geist und Körper, Seele und Leib* (Leipzig: Verlag der Dürr'schen Buchhandlung, 1903), 23, 414.

35. Reinke, *Die Welt als That*, 259.

he gives the impression that only "cosmic reason" [*kosmische Vernunft*] should be accepted in accounting for organic beings and that the unchangeable laws of nature are bound to and limited by it. [This cosmic reason] seems not to be a creator of all things but rather a "cosmic watchmaker" [*Weltuhrmacher*], "the supreme cause in relation to the existence of organisms" [*die oberste Ursache in Bezug auf das Dasein der Organismen*].[36] Others postulate a yet smaller circle of operations from the teleological principle. Although a telos is impossible without consciousness, and reason's mastery of the world cannot be proved, L. Stein[37] argues that it is possible first to speak of a telos when a conscious, organic being appears in the world, meaning there is thus no transcendent but only immanent teleology.[38]

But this view is so dualistic that it satisfies no one in the long term. Nature and history cannot be separated in this manner and set in enmity against each other. Considered from the viewpoint of logic, the mechanical worldview should deserve preference, because it avoids such a division in the world and such a break in our thinking.

But the theory that the world could be understood as a machine is nothing but weak prejudice. Knowledge

---

36. Reinke, *Die Welt als That*, 297.

37. Ludwig Stein (1859–1930) was a Hungarian-born, German-educated Jewish philosopher who advanced a theory of optimistic social progress rooted in the notion of messianic redemption. Cf. Jacob Haberman, "Ludwig Stein: Rabbi, Professor, Publicist, and Philosopher of Evolutionary Optimism," *Jewish Quarterly Review* 86, no. 1/2 (July–October 1995), 91–125.—Ed.

38. Ludwig Stein, *An der Wende des Jahrhunderts* (Freiburg: J. T. B. Mohr, 1899), 17.

acquired in physics and chemistry, which only concerns a comparatively small portion of reality, is piecework; it bounces around the limits of knowledge. Nature in its simpler, inorganic phenomena offers science the same problems, according to Nägeli, as the emergence of perception and consciousness does.[39] Research in chemistry in recent years has shown as clearly as possible that the world of small things is just as wondrous as the world of great things and is full of puzzles and mysteries for the open-minded observer. The very smallest body that can be perceived by strong magnification is a world in itself, and the atoms, formerly regarded as so simple, seem to be as internally puzzling as the stars above.[40] And the world's secrecy increases when we move from the lifeless to the living, from matter to spirit, from nature to history. This richness of being, of which the unknown outnumbers the known a thousandfold, makes a mockery of the explanation of a machine composed of atoms.

It is only when we exchange the mechanical and dynamic worldview for the organic that justice is done to both the oneness and diversity, and equally to being and becoming.[41] According to this organic worldview, the world is in no sense one-dimensional; rather, it contains a fullness of being, a rich exchange of phenomena, a rich

---

39. Hertwig, *Die Entwicklung der Biologie*, 27–28.

40. Johannes Wilhelm Classen, *Naturwissenschaftliche Erkenntnis und der Glaube an Gott* (Hamburg: Boysen, 1903).

41. On the concept of "organic" and "mechanical," see Rudolf Eucken, *Geistige Strömungen der Gegenwart* (Leipzig: Veit, 1904), 125–50.

multiplicity of creations. This "diversity of things is the prerequisite of the whole world process, in that the same process ought to give rise to something that it was not in the beginning."[42] There are lifeless and living, inorganic and organic, inanimate and animate, unconscious and conscious, material and spiritual creations, which differ, respectively, in character but are still taken up in the one-ness of the whole.

This organic view has this over the mechanical: it is more capacious in heart and broader in vision. The mechanical view is exclusive; it demands the whole world for itself. But the organic view also recognizes the mechanical explanation's good right over its own terrain and within the limits imposed by nature itself. It only opposes the a priori demand that life, consciousness, freedom, and telos must be explained mechanically, on the grounds that any other explanation would be unscientific. If a scientific researcher regards the mechanical explanation of life as impossible and then flees to the vitality hypothesis, he is, formally, equally entitled to this view—regardless of the material soundness of his hypothesis—as is someone else who decides, because of the phenomena he perceives, for atoms or dynamides, for the powers of laws. This has nothing to do with dualistic supranaturalism. Soul

---

42. Gustav Portig, *Das Weltgesetz des kleinsten Kraftaufwandes in den Reichen der Natur*, vol. 1, *In der Mathematik, Physik und Chemie* (Stuttgart: Kielmann, 1903), cited in *Beweis des Glaubens* (September–October 1904): 259. [Bavinck gives the quotation in German: "Verschiedenheit der Dinge ist die Voraussetzung des ganzen Weltprozesses, wenn derzelbe etwas bewirken soll, was es selbst anfangs nicht ist."—Ed.]

and life, consciousness and freedom, spirit and thought are just as much phenomena as matter and force are in nature as we perceive them, and they have a right to be explained.[43]

The organic view thus acknowledges and proceeds from the multiplicity of creations, just as nature itself shows us. It does not approach nature with a theory but rather takes it as it gives itself to us. It does not limit the concept of nature and does not let its limits merge with those of physics, it does not identify the causal with the mechanical order, and it does not press physical phenomena into a straitjacket in a predetermined system. But in this multiplicity, it also accepts fully the oneness and harmony in which the world is perceived. While the mechanical view lets the world fall apart objectively in atoms and subjectively in perceptions, and thus can never achieve anything but an accidental, nominalistic unity, the organic view proceeds from the whole to the parts, from the unity to the multiplicity. In reality, there are only two world-views, the theistic and the atheistic, because the question posed by this division is always, Which has priority—spirit or matter, thinking or being, word or "deed," the conscious or the unconscious, God or the world? Whether one calls reason, spirit, or will the cause of all things, it makes no difference when the characteristics of that cause are denied to the absolute by embracing pantheism. And

---

43. Von Hartmann, "Mechanismus und Vitalismus in der modernen Biologie," 345; von Hartmann, *Philosophie des Unbewussten*, 3:vi.

to this question, the Christian—that is, the organic—view gives the answer that thinking proceeds from being, word precedes deed. All things are knowable because they were first thought. And because they are first thought, they can be distinct and still one. It is the idea that animates and protects the organism's distinct parts.[44]

The question regarding the priority of thinking turns back on every part of the creation, from the simplest phenomena to the most complicated. It arises upon consideration of the final components of things. With the heathen, matter was always a godless thing, something that existed eternally in a formless state and that always stood in opposition to the dominance of the idea. But the Christian doctrine of creation, incarnation, and resurrection made this dualism impossible in principle. Matter also has its origin in God and does not stand as an unruly power against him. Rather, it is wholly dependent on him and subject to his will. Yes, because it is wholly from and through God, Thomas did not go wrong when he said that it has a certain resemblance to the divine Being.[45] And although it forms no opposition to God because of its origin, it cannot be dualistically—without any connection—separated from all that is spirit. It is true that one formerly accepted the reality not only of material

44. Friedrich Adolf Trendelenburg, *Logische Untersuchungen* (Leipzig: Hirzel, 1862), 2:17, 19, 124.

45. Thomas Aquinas, *Summa Theologiae* 1a.14.11: "Materia, licet recedat a Dei, similitudine secundum suam potentialitatem, tamen inquantum vel sic esse habet, similitudinem quendam retinet divini esse."

substance but also of spiritual substance. Nonetheless, both, although distinct in essence, were brought forth by one and the same divine wisdom and thus did not stand in opposition to each other. Furthermore, they were intimately linked and closely bound. Both were taken up in one nature. Descartes was the first to break this harmony of soul and body, exchanging it for an antithesis, which the philosophy of the present age has caused to stray to the right or the left and which now lives again in psychophysical parallelism.

There is not only distinction in being, in the substance, but much more so in *being in a certain way*, in the form and figure of things. Throughout the whole world, we see that being is bound up with becoming and becoming with being. The typical, the general, the sort remains; one does not perceive grapes from thorns or figs from thistles; a plant does not become an animal or an animal a human or a human an angel. This is, as Liebmann[46] rightly says, the truth of Platonism. And yet we also see the whole world, with all that it contains, in constant movement; there is an unbroken emergence and departure, a restlessly born becoming and dying; no creature is like another, or even fully like itself, for two moments. The only thing permanent here below is impermanence. That is the truth in Darwinism.[47]

---

46. Otto Liebmann (1840–1912) was a German neo-Kantian philosopher.—Ed.
47. Otto Liebmann, *Zur Analysis der Wirklichkeit* (Strasbourg: Trübner, 1900), 318; Liebmann, *Gedanken und Thatsachen*, 2:142.

These are the facts that stand firm for everyone. To
deny them or to sacrifice one series of them for another
is of no benefit. The concept of evolution has recalled
Heraclitus's *panta rei* ["everything flows"] and denied
the reality of the general, of the class. But a large-scale
return to Aristotle's *formae substantiales* can now be
detected. Hans Driesch[48] says in the foreword to his most
recent work that he intends a synthesis of Aristotelian
and Newtonian "principles of research" [*Forschungs-
maximen*] and calls the newest turn in science "a return
to substantial forms and the hidden qualities of Aristotle and the scholastics, all of which had been thought
overcome."[49] However great the variability might be,
heredity is so constant that the process of development
cannot be understood without directing thoughts and
formative powers. As researchers in the natural sciences
and philosophers have recently begun to speak again
of the efficiency of the unconscious, of the mute will, of
ensouled atoms, of a special life force, of "dominant
designs" [*Gestaltungsdominanten*], of "heterogony of
ends" [*Heterogenie der Zwecke*], of a "capacity for
effective adaptation" [*Fähigkeit der zweckmässigen
Anpassung*],[50] and so forth, this shows a more or less
openhearted appreciation that matter and energy are in-

---

48. Hans Driesch (1867–1941) was a German biologist and philosopher.—Ed.

49. Driesch, *Naturbegriffe und Natururteile*, iv, 53, 224; Liebmann, *Gedanken
und Thatsachen*, 2:149. [Bavinck gives the quotation in German: "Zurück zu den
für überwunden gehaltenen substanziellen Formen und verborgenen Eigenschaften
des Aristoteles und der Scholastik."—Ed.]

50. Von Hartmann, "Mechanismus und Vitalismus in der modernen Biologie."

sufficient to explain things in their being or in their *being in a certain way.*

Scripture also teaches not only that creaturely substance is distinctive but that the same substance is organized differently in different creatures. A particular character has been gifted to heaven and earth, sun, moon and stars, to plants, animals, humans, and so on, through which they—individually or in their generations—remain what they are. Scripture makes no definitive statement on whether matter leads to many or few elements or also to a single final element; neither does it give us a catalog of immutable sorts that would resemble our usual distinctions; but it does show us that not only being but also *being in a certain way* is defined by God in both substance and organization. Led by this, Christian philosophy could also appropriate the Platonic-Aristotelian doctrine of ideas, the forms, in a modified sense. Indeed, we cannot arrive at the account of things without such forms. But these forms are not to be handled as, in the Kantian sense, categories that we apply to the matter of perception by our spiritual industry. They are, rather, neither something subjective alone nor something passive that is carried into the material of our perception. But they are to be considered objective ideas, which give order and coherence to the multiplicity of parts and bind them in an organic unity. They make things into what each is in its own particularity. Just as an artist lays down his idea in the marble, so God realizes his word in the world. Herein, however, lies this great distinction. Humans can make only works or art or instruments, which are always transcended—more or less—by the idea. God, however, creates beings that, while remaining instruments in his hands (Isa. 10:15), nonetheless absorb the idea and realize themselves through spontaneous activity. A thought does not float upward; rather, it is already present in things. In a certain sense, this is true of all creatures and of the whole world. The whole world can, in the right sense, be called an organism, a ζῷον ["a living creature"],[51] although we may not yet assign a living soul to monads, atoms, or stars (as with Leibniz,[52] Haeckel, or Fechner[53]) on that basis. The whole universe is a revelation of divine wisdom. God is not only transcendent above, he is also immanent in all that is created by his Word and Spirit.

By this, the following observation deserves to be made: The divine wisdom explains the essence of things, their oneness and their distinction, but not their existence. Being does not follow from thought alone. Against intellectualism, voluntarism stands its ground on the basis that not the thought but rather only the will can be the *principium existendi* ["principle of existing"] of things. Ideas can be the *causae exemplares* ["model causes"], but being alone can be no *causa efficiens* ["efficient cause"].

---

51. Tilmann Pesch, *Die grossen Welträthsel* (Berlin: Herder, 1907), 1:46, 50; Liebmann, *Gedanken und Thatsachen*, 2:177.

52. Gottfried Wilhelm Leibniz (1646–1716) was a German rationalist philosopher who made contributions to many fields, including mathematics, physics, and ethics.—Ed.

53. Gustav Fechner (1801–1887) was a German physicist and philosopher who helped found the discipline of psychophysics.—Ed.

The word must be joined by the deed, generation must be joined by creation, wisdom must be joined by God's decree, in order to grant a real existence to what existed eternally in the divine consciousness as an idea. The agreement between the teachings of Scripture and Platonism, between the doctrine of wisdom and the logos doctrine of the Bible, on the one hand, and the logos speculation of Greek philosophy, on the other, may not overlook their great distinction. According to Scripture, ideas have no objective, metaphysical existence outside God but rather exist only in his divine being. They contain neither the general concepts, the types and forms of things, nor the thoughts of all that shall be or happen (without the slightest exception), and they are not realized by themselves or by an "artisan" [δημιουργός] who has taken it as a model. Rather, they are realized by God's will from his own consciousness. It is through the divine will, which is thought-led, the "counsel of [God's] will" [βολην τον θελήματος], which grants things their existence and makes them persist therein. God's thoughts, spoken in his Word, in his Son, are the *causae exemplares* of things, the band between God and world, between the one and the many. But they are taken into the things themselves by the will, by the power of God, and created in them as *immanente causae* ["immanent causes"]. God grants existence to all things in the Son (Col. 1:15),[54] and the

---

54. Bavinck incorrectly cites Col. 1:15; the reference should be Col. 1:16.—Ed.

Son bears up all things by the word of his power (Heb. 1:3). By this will, by this power of God, it can be understood that the thoughts of things become active *principia* in them and animate and govern them as "the beginning of movement" [ἀρχαι της κινησεως]. The old saying *forma dat esse rei* ["the form gives existence to the thing"] must therefore be understood properly. Only formally is it true that the *forma* gives the *materia* its *essentia, distinctio, operatio*. In the effective sense, this is all due to God's will.[55] Divine "power" [δυναμις], divine "energy" [ἐνεργεια], is active in the world, and through this, things are and work. Divine energy is the source of all powers and energies in the creatures, and because this divine energy is not blind but is rather led by divine wisdom, the powers and workings in the natural world also demonstrate direction and course. They are not externally coerced, but rather, internally, in their own being, they are bound to thought.

This doctrine of God's wisdom and will also explains the development that is to be perceived throughout the world. The advocates of the mechanical view do indeed speak of development and advancement, of evolution and progress, but they do not think deeply into these concepts and are satisfied with mere sounds. If this were not the case, they would easily see that development—in the sense of progress and perfection—cannot be united with

---

55. Alsted, *Encyclopaedia*, 1:615.

a machine made up of atoms. From that standpoint, these questions are prone to being unanswerable:

> How should perfection, higher civilization, ascendancy, perfectibility, by the same continuous—either anarchic or ochlocratic—soulless machine composed of atoms, be imaginable? Why does nature not eternally remain a chaotic swirl of dust and foggy mist but rather, through physical and chemical mechanics of atoms, provide eyes that see, ears that hear, nerves that feel, muscles that bend and stretch, brains capable of thought, and ultimately a logic, a reason, an ethics? How can nature do that?[56]

In the mechanical worldview, there is no place for development in the actual sense. All differences between things, however great, are ultimately accidental and quantitative. Nothing *becomes*, because there is nothing that *needs* to become, that *must* become. There is no goal and no starting point—and development is based precisely on both of these things. It describes the path that leads from the one to the other. It is possible only when things are something, when they have a "nature," a *principium* ["principle"] and *radix* ["root"] of all their

---

56. Liebmann, *Gedanken und Thatsachen*, 2:142. [Bavinck gives the quotation in German: "Wie Vervollkommnung, Höherbildung, Emporgang, Perfectibilität bei durchgängig gleicher, anarchischer oder ochlokratischer, zielloser Mechanik der Atome denkbar sein soll? Wie kommt denn die Natur dazu, nicht ewig ein chaotischer Staubwirbel und Dunstnebel zu bleiben, sondern sich durch physikalische und chemische Mechänik der Atome sehende Augen, hörende Ohren, fühlende Nerven, beugende und streckende Muskeln, denkfähige Gehirne, schliesslich eine Logik, eine Vernunft, eine Ethik zu verschaffen? Wie kann sie das."—Ed.]

attributes and activities, and when they, by virtue of that nature, must become something and have to meet a destination. There is thus no development in machines and instruments. It is found only in organic beings, be they material or spiritual, because although it may be that matter and spirit are distinguished by essence, a *materia* also pertains to the created spiritual beings, in that they are also composed "from potency and actuality, genre and difference, being and essence."[57] God alone is absolute being, the "I will be who I will be," but all creatures—including the pneumatic and the psychic—are subject to the law of becoming. They must and they can become, because they are something, because they have a nature, a *forma*, that masters them and leads them in a particular direction. This nature is, as it were, the "divine sound" [θειος φωνη] that "reverberates in every body" [*sonas in quolibet corpore*], the "power of God in ordinary things" [*vis Dei ordinaria rebus insita*].[58] But because it is the divine wisdom and power that works in all things, it is possible to speak of development in relation to the world, in its totality. It is true that this world contains many inanimate, lifeless things, of which, in the strict sense, there can be no talk of development, but these are still taken up as organic parts in the totality of the world, and that totality of the world is an organ-

---

57. Alsted, *Encyclopaedia*, 1:681, 643. [Bavinck gives the quotation in Latin: "ex potentia et actu, genere et differentia, ente et essential."—Ed.]

58. Alsted, *Encyclopaedia*, 1:676.

ism that develops according to firm laws and strives toward a goal. From the viewpoint of the mechanical worldview, this belief has no right to exist. Then, there is nothing but an eternal *panta rei* ["everything flows"], a monotone undulation in the ocean of being: nothing is reached and nothing acquired; if this world has passed away, there remains only a place for the despairing question, What was all this for?[59] In the organic worldview, it is the opposite: the Christian worldview gives us the right to speak of a development in all things and pertaining to the entire world, because here is a divine thought that must be realized in the passing of time. God has created all things for his own will. He makes all things subservient to the honor of his name. From him and through him and to him are all things.[60]

In whatever manner and according to whichever laws this development—in the whole as much as in the parts— takes place, a great deal is hidden from us. Chemistry has probed deeper than ever into the nature, the affinity, the connections between elements. With the help of acute,

59. Friedrich von Hellwald, *Kulturgeschichte in ihrer natürlichen entwicklung bis zur gegenwart* (Augsburg: Lampart, 1883), 2:727.
60. The idea of development is discussed, among other places, in my work *Schepping of Ontwikkeling* (Kampen: J. H. Kok, 1901), 39; and among others, Pesch, *Die grossen Welträthsel*, 2:128; Heinrich Pesch, *Liberalismus, Socialismus und Christliche Gesellschaftsordnung* (Freiburg: Herder, 1901), 3:257; Max Reischle, "Wissenschaftliche Entwicklungserforschung und evolutionistische Weltanschauung in ihrem Verhältnis zum Christentum," *Zeitschrift für Theologie und Kirche* 12, no. 1 (1902): 1–43; Abraham Kuyper, *Evolutie* (Amsterdam: Hoveker en Wormser, 1899); Ambrosius Arnold Willem Hubrecht, *De evolutie in nieuwe banen* (Utrecht: J. van Druten, 1902); Max Heinze, "Evolutionismus," in *Realencyklopädie für protestantische Theologie und Kirche* (Graz: Akademische Druck- u. Verlagsanstalt, 1896–1913), 3:627–81; Eucken, *Geistige Strömungen der Gegenwart*, 185; etc.

invented instruments, and through precise experimental research, physiology has granted us much better knowledge than before of the functions of organisms, such as breathing, blood circulation, digestion, metabolism, the formation of blood, the workings of sensory organs and the brain, and so on. Botanists and zoologists have peered into the signs of life of the cell, the protoplasma, and the nucleus. The process of insemination, in its every stage, has been followed and determined by microscopic research. All this study, however, has not yet led to a firm result. There are as many hypotheses on the origin of reproduction as there are researchers; the one seems to be more untenable than the other.[61] Only vitalism has gained some influence in recent times.[62] In the battle currently waged between preformation [*praeformatie*] and epigenesis, between vitalism and antivitalism, between teleology and (mechanical) causality, between immanent and transcendent teleology, the principal question is always this: whether the formation of the organism falls under the dominion of an immaterial principle, that is, it is governed by an idea; or whether it happens only "according to blind laws of necessity" [*nach blinden Gesetzen der Nothwendigkeit*], that is, the organism is the principle or product of its changes.[63]

---

61. Kuyper, *Evolutie*, 27–32.
62. Von Hartmann, "Mechanismus und Vitalismus in der modernen Biologie," 369–77.
63. Theodor Schwann cited in Otto, "Die mechanistische Lebenstheorie und die Theologie," 179–213.

Although science is currently wholly committed to its preference for understanding the organism in the last sense, mechanically, people were formerly led by the desire to understand it in a mechanical-organic manner. The concept of generation thus had a far broader meaning than in the present day, when it is applied to all organic beings. Then, generation was spoken of in relation to all lifeless creations—for example, to meteors "generated by the rising vapors" [*quae ex elevatis vaporibus generantur*]—and indicated a full sense of becoming in so doing.[64] A great deal of ignorance was doubtless at play in this; when, as was often the case, one did not know the physical cause of some change, one provided a metaphysical explanation for it. When the limits between the organic and the inorganic were not strictly divided, one often attributed "an invisible element" [*elementum invisible*], "a spirit" [*spiritus*], "a star" [*astrum*], to the inanimate. And when matter and body were considered dead and inert, one attributed all working to "a hidden architect" [*faber occultus*], the archeus, "an entity of seed and power" [*ens seminis et virtutis*].[65] To the contrary, more recent science has shown that the domination of the mechanical is far more extensive than was formerly believed, even in organic chemistry, and it has even gained ground from the organism in the realm of physiology. According to the laws of optometry, the eye is designed as a *camera*

---

64. Alsted, *Encyclopaedia*, 1:677.
65. Alsted, *Encyclopaedia*, 1:692–93.

obscura;[66] the ear is a cultured acoustic instrument; the blood circulation system is subject to the same hydrostatic laws as any other liquid. Wöhler[67] has even discovered that "urea" [*Harnstoff*] was an artificially created connection, following which others succeeded in forming numerous carbon compounds—which had long been regarded as products of life force [*producten der levenskracht*].[68]

But this does not remove the fact that in generation, just as was formerly understood, a principle—which is of great significance for the organic worldview and which is confirmed by the newer science—lurks. Chemistry continually teaches that there are connections between all affine elements. Synthesis is not random but rather is bound by laws; it assumes a defined quality and quantity of elements. It is not the case that all things are connectable or are so to the same extent. There is order and rule also in this process. Furthermore, the thing that emerges through connection is old but also new. A body that emerges in this way has different attributes than each of the parts that have been bound together has. Bodies put together by chemistry are different from their chemical components. Water is essentially distinguished from hydrogen and oxygen, taken on their own. Sulfuric acid is something different from sulfur or oxygen. Just as the word *soul* forms its

---

66. Bavinck is comparing the eye to a darkened enclosure, such as a pinhole camera or dark room, with a small hole enabling light to enter, which projects an image from one surface onto the opposite surface.—Ed.

67. Friedrich Wöhler (1800–1882) was a noted nineteenth-century German chemist.—Ed.

68. Hertwig, *Die Entwicklung der Biologie*, 19–20.

own distinctive sound, which is not identical to each of its individually pronounced letters, so is each chemical connection something different and something higher than can be understood in each of the elements bound.[69] In synthesis, each element decodes—to a certain extent—its own existence and character. Finally, because one can create this connection of elements artificially, and likewise their separation, one makes clear that one knows and understands this process. To establish a fact, however, is wholly other than explaining and understanding it. Each chemical element is a mystery, in the fullest sense, in its being, attributes, and workings. The smallest body that can be made visible is a world in itself: in their nature, atoms and molecules, dynamides and energies remain wholly unknown to us. To a certain extent, we can establish laws, according to which one phenomenon follows another, but "that which takes place inwardly . . . by which hidden processes effect transitions from one phenomenon to the other, eternally remains a mystery to us."[70] And the chemical binding of elements remains equally mysterious, as does the new thing produced by that combination.

Now to be analogous is certainly not to be identical. Nonetheless, it remains clear that in the realm of the inorganic, we are confronted by the same problem

---

69. Joseph Kleutgen, *Die Philosophie der Vorzeit* (Münster: Theissing, 1860), 2:314–35.

70. Classen, *Naturwissenschaftliche Erkenntnis und der Glaube an Gott*, 18. [Bavinck gives the quotation in German: "was dabei im Innern . . . sich vollzieht, durch welche verborgene Vorgänge der Uebergang von der einen Erscheinung zur andern sich vollzieht, das bleibt für uns ewig ein Geheimniss."—Ed.]

that occurs in the realm of the organic: generation. In whichever manner this happens, from this binding we always see something new coming forth, which cannot be explained mechanically, by addition alone. For this reason, in former times one spoke of generation in all becoming. This supports the binding of affine elements, the pairing of related things. It follows elements that unite, as "form" [*forma*] and "matter" [*materia*], heredity and variability, a centripetal and centrifugal force, sperm and egg, the male and female elements. Each semen develops only in "a suitable womb" [*conveniens matrix*], "which is like a divine sacred reservoir" [*quae est divina veluti favissa*],[71] and it brings forth something new by falling into the earth and dying: "the corruption of one is the generation of the other" [*corruptio unius est generatio alterius*] (John 12:24).

Development exists, therefore, not only in gradual, ongoing transformation, "motion" [*motus*], but just as was formerly accepted[72] and is now demonstrated again by Prof. Hugo de Vries,[73] in a great leap, an acute mutation, which is to say, in a "redesign that is uncreated, as it were, suddenly emerging from the endless fullness of creative freedom."[74] And so, development—which is built

---

71. Alsted, *Encyclopaedia*, 1:693.

72. Leonhard Schmöller, *Die Scholastische Lehre von Materie und Form* (Passau: Kleiter, 1903), 15, 19.

73. Hugo de Vries (1848–1935) was a Dutch botanist and pioneer in the field of genetics.—Ed.

74. Ludwig Kuhlenbeck, *Natürliche Grundlagen des Rechts und der Politik* (Eisenach: Thüringische Verlags-Anstalt, 1904), 54. [Bavinck gives the quotation in

on the organic worldview—shows itself to be a development that advances and makes each part of the whole, and the whole itself, approach its final goal, which God has established for it.

The organic worldview is, therefore, finally teleological through and through. It is not so in the flat sense of rationalism, which considers human understanding as the measure and goal of all things. Rather, it is so in the elevated sense that Scripture makes known to us and according to which everything exists through God and for his glory. This teleology is in no way at all at odds with the causal link that we notice everywhere in nature and history. "Nothing comes from nothing" [*ex nihilo nihil fit*] and "no effect without cause" [*nullus effectus sine causa*] are logical rules opposed by nobody. But there are different sorts of causes. Teleology is at odds not with the causal but rather with the mechanical view, because it knows no nature but the bodily, no substance but the material, no power but the physical, and therefore also no cause but the mechanical. It wants to compress the richness of the created in its own single, dauntingly narrow-minded system, even as the creation shows itself in its endless variety of substances and powers, of causes and laws. Newton believed the "ideas" [*formae*] of things could be exchanged for laws. But this is not so, and the aforementioned return to the "substantial forms"

German: "unschöpferischen, gewissermassen aus der unendlichen Fülle der schöpferischen Freiheit unvermittelt auftauchenden Neugestaltung."—Ed.]

[*formae substantiales*] now shines sufficient light on this. Ideas and laws are different. Ideas express created things' manners of *being*, and laws, their manners of *moving* and *functioning*. Created things *function* differently, to the degree that they *are* different. Whoever loses sight of this distinction runs the risk of hypostatizing the laws as Plato did the ideas and of allowing them to hover above the things, like demonic powers.[75] Because created things differ from each other in idea and character, however, they move and function according to different laws. These are different for machines and organisms, for the physical and psychic, for nature and history, for head and heart, for the rational and the moral life. Even the realm of the miraculous is governed by a discrete thought and law.

All these different created things, with their different substances, ideas, powers, and laws, are—according to the organic view—taken up in one great whole and are subservient to an ultimate goal. There is finality everywhere, in the inorganic and in the organic. That we often do not see this reality demonstrates that it is indeed there, where we do indeed see it. But this finality presses causality everywhere into its service. Just as the one who sets a certain goal then uses the means and goes down the paths necessary to reach it, so do "final causes" [*causae finales*] everywhere use "efficient causes" [*causae efficientes*] to realize themselves. The former, therefore, are the true

---

75. Otto Willmann, *Geschichte des Idealismus* (Braunschweig: F. Vieweg und Sohn, 1896), 3:215.

causes, the actual driving forces, and the latter set the
conditions without which they cannot be realized. Darwinism, as far as it contains the truth, can—at most—set
the conditions, or show us the occasional causes, under
which and through which development takes place, but
it still owes us an answer to the questions of why and for
what it happens.[76] Darwin does not provide us with that
answer; neither does Plato or Aristotle. It is only provided
by the Christian confession that God is the Creator and
that his glory is the goal of all things. Everything is subservient to this. Everything is directed to it.

Considered in this way, "final causes" [*causae finales*]
are neither mischievous enemies or strange intruders who
ambush the actual causes from outside and force them—
against their will—into submission. They are, however,
the formative and leading *principia* in the things themselves, the energies upheld by divine power, which the
created things bring forth on the path of development
and which give direction to their movement. With this,
there is a very certain distinction in grade and measure, in
which the different created things' "purposeful thought"
[*Zweckgedanke*] is immanent. There is, according to K. E.
von Baer, a "determination" [*Zielstrebigkeit*] and an "ex-
pediency" [*Zweckmässigkeit*]; there is transcendent and
immanent teleology.[77] For the machine, the goal it serves

---

76. Liebmann, *Zur Analysis der Wirklichkeit*, 354; Liebmann, *Gedanken and Thatsachen*, 2:163.
77. Trendelenburg, *Logische Untersuchungen*, 2:29, 30.

always remains something inwardly strange. But to the extent that the created things exist organically, the "final cause" [*causa finalis*] is taken up within them as idea, and they work together for its realization.[78] And viewed from the highest standpoint, the whole world is an organic unity, upheld by one thought, led by one will, directed to one goal—one "organon" [ὀργανον] that is also a "machine" [μηχανη] and a "machine" [μηχανη] that is also an "organon" [ὀργανον], a *building* that *grows* and a *body* that is *built*. It is a work of art from the Supreme Artist and from the Master Builder of the universe.

---

78. Trendelenburg, *Logische Untersuchungen*, 2:79.

3

Becoming and Acting

The harmony of this worldview [*wereldbeeld*], however, is interrupted by the sharp contrasts to which we are introduced especially in relation to the third problem, that between becoming and acting [*handelen*]. Is there, in the stream of occurrences, still a place for personal, independent, and free acting? Can we on good grounds and in confidence continue to say, "I think, I will, I act," or is Lichtenberg's word true: "Should one say, 'It thinks,' just as one says, 'It is raining'?"[1] Is the impersonal, neutral

1. Here Bavinck refers to the work of Georg Christoph Lichtenberg (1742–1799), the German physicist and satirist. Lichtenberg's original quote asks whether people should speak about their own actions using the same (German) grammatical constructions employed to discuss phenomena beyond the self—in this case, the weather ("Es denkt, sollte man sagen, wie man sagt, es blitzt?"). While Lichtenberg refers to lightning ("es blitzt," literally, "it lightnings") rather than rain, differing

"it" of theosophy the only and all-propelling power, or does the scheme of things allow space for personality and freedom? Is there only *physis* ["nature"], or is there also *ethos* ["character"]?

As soon as we attempt to think about this question, we are stopped by this remarkable and undeniable fact, that where in reality we are free, we are in any case unable to find freedom to not be free. The reality, the possibility even, of freedom is contestable, but the right and duty toward freedom is indisputable. We are not free in order simply to lay ourselves down passively before events and let ourselves be carried along, carefree, by the stream of life.[2] For as soon as we awaken to consciousness, we discover that there are laws and norms above us that direct us in order to elevate us above nature and force us to release from its coercion.[3] In these norms, another world—different and higher than is revealed to us in nature—makes itself known to us. It is a world not of obligation [*moeten*] but of belonging [*behoren*], of ethical freedom and choice. In these norms, a moral world order in the midst of and above empirical reality is maintained, a world of ideas, of truth, goodness, and beauty. Though it is the case that it despises all coercion, this world order

---

ways of describing meteorological phenomena in English and German require a dynamic translation to convey Lichtenberg's point.—Ed.

2. Otto Liebmann, *Gedanken und Thatsachen* (Strasbourg: Trübner, 1901), 2:179.

3. In the article, "De wereldbeschouwing van een Nederlandsch wijsgeer," *Onze Eeuw* (October 1905): 129–57, van der Wijck discusses Prof. Heijmans's *Einführung in die Metaphysik* and remarks that Prof. Heijmans speaks only of laws and not of norms, while the question of causality or normality is still of greater importance than that of the question of the physical or psychical.

in its moral character possesses a power surpassing that of nature. The question is not about whether humans can or want to obey its laws; it says categorically that it is appropriate to do so. You shall love the true, the good, and the beautiful with all your soul; and you shall love God above all else and then your neighbor as yourself.

This phenomenon is strikingly majestic. Everywhere in the world, strict causality prevails; nothing occurs by chance; everything has a cause. But in the moral order of the world, a power appears before us that seems to take no account of this causality. It accepts no appeals to our powerlessness and ignorance, has no appetite for excuses or facile explanations, and will not settle for good intentions or solemn promises; it does not negotiate with the conscience. But it demands that we all, without exception, always and everywhere, in all circumstances of life, conform ourselves to its command. Truth, goodness, and beauty lay claim to the whole person and never release us from its service. The human being must follow the moral ideal and be perfect, as is the Father of humanity, who is in heaven, [and he must be this] not merely at the end of a long maturation but now, in this moment, and always. And as such, we recognize, as if it were instinctive, the fairness of the demand, by which we ourselves continually judge others. We are not apathetic spectators of what takes place around us, but we test everything by the law of the true, the good, and the beautiful and pronounce our agreement or disagreement. When this concerns ourselves, self-interest usually provides us with many ready excuses. But when it comes to other people, we almost never apply these [same excuses]. We uphold before them the strictest standards, and we demand, if not in theory then in practice, if not in abstraction then in each concrete case, that they should have been different and should have acted differently than they were and had acted. As such, we do not rest in empirical reality and are not satisfied by causal explanations. We bear within us a law, which accuses us that we should be and act differently than we actually are and do act. We form value judgments; we believe in ideal goods; we hold fast to imperishable, eternal norms.

Where do these norms come from? Are they a self-deception? Are they one chapter in the pathology of the human spirit, akin to witchcraft and the delusions of the insane? For as long as the existence of God was firmly established in the human consciousness, this question could not arise. By his existence, the origin of all authority and law was declared. But when modern science arose and emancipated itself from all faith and religion, the foundation of all law, even the moral law, was destabilized. Supernaturalism and rationalism still tried with physics and all kinds of theology to maintain the old position but proved weak against the attack. At that time, Kant emerged and sought another, firmer foundation for the moral law in the essence of human nature. To that end, he first pointed science to her limits. For in order to obtain a place for faith, he first had to deprive knowing of a large part of its terrain. Indeed, in Kant's view, the intellect is bound to empirical reality and cannot rise above it. It knows nothing of unseen and eternal things. It can obtain no certainty about God, the soul, and immortality: if a person had nothing apart from reason, he would know nothing about these things. But yet, he still has practical reason, a heart, and a conscience, and herein he feels bound to an absolute law, to an ideal norm. This moral bond is grounded in human nature; it is an a priori that cannot be derived from experience. Kant works from this given: the absolute validity of the obligation is, to him, the basis of morality, theology, and religion. Philosophy, driven out from the domain of science, receives the task of research into the assessment of necessary, generally applicable values.[4]

By returning to the absolute, unconditional validity of duty, Kant performed an outstanding service for morality in his day. There is also no doubt that Kant was animated by an intense effort to hold ideal norms, in their superiority, high above human approval and self-interest. But the question remains whether he succeeded in giving morality a new foundation, which was destined for

---

4. Wilhelm Windelband, *Praludiën: Aufsätze und Reden zur Philosophie und ihrer Geschichte*, 2nd ed. (Tübingen: Mohr, 1903), 1–57, 119–54; Windelband, *Immanuel Kant und seine Weltanschauung* (Heidelberg: Winter, 1904). A considerable difference of opinion exists regarding the question of the extent to which Kant maintained metaphysics. Compare A. Bruining, "Kant en het Rationalisme," *Nieuw Theologisch Tijdschrift* (1912): 217–45; Bruining, "Kants kennisleer en de wijsgeerige Theologie," *Nieuw Theologisch Tijdschrift* (1912): 392–421.

criticism. At first, this appears to be the case. But when the historical sense was awakened in the nineteenth century, and the idea of evolution was applied everywhere in the sciences, many began to doubt whether human nature, with its sense of duty, was indeed an objective and immutable given, from which one could safely proceed in researching the moral life. *Physis* and *ethos*, however, could not be so dualistically separated, as though in one (without exception), the law of causality applied and science could speak, while in the other, the causal bond was terminated in order to create a place for faith. The human being had not simply appeared out of the blue, psychically or physically; he had become historical. The sense of duty and the moral law had gradually formed in him, just as the fact of the great difference that exists between humans and peoples of one time and of another conclusively proves: the human, as a moral being, was a product of his environment. Besides, Kant was of the opinion that the sense of duty and the moral law did not need God to explain their origin and essence. He reversed the order, not building morality on religion but rather building religion with theology on morality. And this was his endeavor, to explain the moral life solely and exclusively from the human being and apart from God. Kant made man autonomous and his own lawgiver. Just as this human creates the phenomenal world through innate conceptual representations and categories of understanding, he also establishes moral order through the idiosyncratic apparatus of his "practical reason" [*praktische Vernunft*]. Now this principle of autonomy in regard to morality seemed to come into its own when it discarded its individualism and was conceived of historically: it is humanity that gradually, in the process of evolution, grants existence and general legitimacy to the moral life, to authority and the sense of duty, to altruistic instincts and ethical motivations.[5]

Against Kant, this criticism was right to a large extent. It fought him with the weapons he himself had wielded. Also, this historical viewpoint had a great charm by first acquaintance: it recognized gradual development and organic growth and often shed surprising light on religious and ethical phenomena. But its limitless application led, in the end, to a great loss. If all is resolved in the process, then the absolute character of the ideal norms of truth and falsehood, of good and evil, of beauty and the ugly could no longer be maintained, because "a truth for today or tomorrow is an absurdity; what is at all true counts for all time, or rather, it has no connection to time at all."[6] In the dialectical process of ideas, in the gradual evolution of the phenomena, there is no place for the absolute.

---

5. According to Windelband, "Normen und Naturgesetze," in *Praludiën*, 249–86, the life of the soul is also governed by indissoluble laws of nature, and its norms are the rules by which the *value* of necessary happenings are judged. Norms are not originally and essentially distinct from the laws of nature, but they gradually emerge by natural necessity and serve nature as a means by which the human being (as is also necessitated by nature) is elevated to a higher, moral standpoint.

6. Rudolf Eucken, *Geistige Strömungen der Gegenwart* (Leipzig: Veit, 1904), 208. [Bavinck gives the quotation in German: "ein Wahres für heute oder morgen ist ein Unding, was irgend wahr ist, das gilt für alle Zeit oder vielmehr ohne alle Beziehung zur Zeit."—Ed.]

Whoever abandons the life of the spirit [*het geestesleven*] in its entirety to the movement distorts it from the inside out[7] and takes away the possibility of ever building it up again on a firm foundation. Let psychology and history be devoted to the most serious and extensive research. The hope, however, is vain that one shall obtain an ethic if one analyzes human tendencies and actions precisely, or that one shall find the true religion through the practice of religious psychology and the history of religions, or that one could organize a society as long as the social instincts were first studied with precision.[8] From becoming there is no transition to being, if not for the fact that being itself is the underlying ground of becoming.

Because a person always needs some form of stability, however, the grave and in no sense imaginary danger quickly arises that through this one-sided historical viewpoint, he is led to a counterfeit nationalism, to a narrow chauvinism, to a fanaticism about race and instinct. Pan-Germanism, pan-Slavism, and so on, supply the proof of this. After Gobineau[9] and the writer of *Rembrandt als Erzieher* [*Rembrandt as Educator*],[10] H. S. Chamberlain[11]

7. Eucken, *Geistige Strömungen der Gegenwart*, 209.

8. Otto Willmann, *Geschichte des Idealismus* (Braunschweig: F. Vieweg und Sohn, 1896), 3:33v.

9. Count Joseph Arthur de Gobineau (1816–1882) was a French aristocrat who developed the notion of an Aryan "master race."—Ed.

10. Julius Langbehn (1851–1907), author of *Rembrandt als Erzieher*, was a Romantic poet who argued for pan-Germanism based on an account of German national superiority.—Ed.

11. Houston Stewart Chamberlain (1855–1927) was a British-born German philosopher, whose works were influential in the early twentieth-century pan-German *völkisch* movement and later shaped the anti-Semitism of the National Socialist Movement.—Ed.

is the eloquent interpreter of this ideology. The norm was sought in the historical, the ideal identified with reality, the relative exalted to the rank of the absolute. From that pedestal, even the highest and holiest is grasped at: if Jesus still wants to retain some authority over us, he has to put up with being injected into the Aryan tribe. All significant peoples had their own religious founder: the Persians had their Zarathustra, the Indians their Buddha, the Chinese their Confucius, the Jews their Moses, the Greeks their Homer, the Arabians their Muhammad, and the most civilized of the Aryans, the Germans, would not have been able to produce such a personality and had, rather, to go to the school of a people like the Jews! How foolish is the one who believes Jesus was not a Jew, that he was an Aryan, and that the Bible, in which every heretic finds his proof text, gives evidence for the matter. "The German spirit shall heal the world."[12] But that is how the so-called pure historical view turns into the most biased construction of history. If the theory or the system requires it, then the primal human is a wild animal, then the most uncivilized peoples are the representatives of the original human race, then the Babylonians are the masters of the Jews, then Jesus did not come from Israel but from the Aryans. Should the evidence for these statements

---

12. H. S. Chamberlain, *Die Grundlagen des neunzehnten Jahrhunderts* (München: Bruckmann, 1903), 1:209; cf. A. Muller, *Jesus, ein Ariër* (Leipzig: Sängewald, 1904); Johannes Lehmann-Hohenberg, *Naturwissenschaft und Bibel* (Jena: Costenoble, 1904), 3, 113. [Bavinck gives the quotation in German: "Am deutschem Wesen wird dereinst die Welt genesen."—Ed.]

lack proof, historical criticism receives the task of providing it at any cost.

Relativism appears, then, to be impartial, as it wants to know of no fixed norms and claims to be concerned with and to speak of only the concrete, the historical. But it makes the relative itself into the absolute and therefore exchanges true freedom for coercion, real faith for superstition. The worst is not that it comes into contradiction with itself by doing so (because this contradiction is present from the beginning, toward skepticism, and toward itself); acknowledging and justifying itself as truth, it takes over the standpoint of the absolute. Windelband rightly says of this, "Whoever proves relativism destroys it."[13] But the great peril lurks in the fact that this robs the ideal norms of their absolute legitimacy. Autonomy for Kant was a means, badly chosen to be sure but still a means, to uphold the categorical character of "You shall" [*Du Sollst*], but through evolutionistic monism, autonomy becomes a principle that undermines every authority and all law. The human person forms his own religion and morality, his own world-and-life view; the main thing is that he, bound to nothing but himself, might enjoy himself and give a moment of aesthetic enjoyment to others.

Naturally, with this, all moral institutions, all establishments of family and society and state, fall apart. Just as the last components of the knowledge of sensory per-

---

13. Windelband, *Praludiën*, 46. [Bavinck gives the quotation in German: "wer den Relativismus beweist, vernichtet ihn."—Ed.]

ceptions and the last components of the natural world
are atoms or energies, so the family, society, and state are
dissolved into their original elements: individual people
(or, to be more consistent, since individuals are also composed of other things, into instincts, fits of fury, and passion). There are, after all, no objective ideas, no moral
relationships, no longer any fixed orders that hold together and organize these elements. But nevertheless, just
as we cannot go beyond our minds in order to form general concepts and to shape a nature beyond ourselves, so
we are likewise forced by necessity to group individuals
into a society. Moral obligation does not exist there, although physical compulsion does. People join together
through a fictitious agreement or by the compulsion of
circumstances. The general concepts are *nomina*, only
subjectively necessary. Nature is a creation of our mind,
and in the same way, the society is a product of social
instincts.[14] Individualism turns into socialism, autonomy
into heteronomy, nominalism into monism, atomism into
pantheism, anarchy into despotism, the sovereignty of the
people into the power of the state, freedom into the tyr-
anny of the majority, not because of ethical necessity but
rather because of practical motives and economic factors.
Karl Marx understood his time when he discovered a
connection between science and society and for that reason wanted to create a link between the intellectual class

---

14. Cf. Ludwig Stein, "Mechanische und organische Staatsauffassung," *Deutsche Rundschau* (August 1904): 249–63.

[*de denkenden*] and the suffering class [*de lijdenden*]. If no other factors are at work in nature and history than those taken into account by the atomistic or energetic worldview, a society as dreamed of by Marx is still the only ideal. Indeed, modern science has a genetic connection to socialism.

There are, however, factors other than atoms, with their mechanical-chemical forces and laws, and so it is not in theory but in practice that they are recognized by all. No judgment would be possible if we did not believe, whether consciously or unconsciously, in the reality of logical, ethical, and aesthetic norms. In the system of Marx and Engels,[15] for example, this came clearly into the light. According to their theory, all ideas regarding law and politics, religion and ethics, science and art are products of economic development. Being—namely, social being—defines consciousness. As Marx expressed in the preface to his *Critique of Political Economy*, "It is not the consciousness of men that determines their existence but their social existence that determines their consciousness."[16] For all that, Engels later recognized that ideal motives such as love and hate, a sense of justice and ambition exercise influence on people's actions and the proceeding of events. With this, he maintained that in

---

15. Friedrich Engels (1820–1895) was a German philosopher and social scientist who collaborated closely with Karl Marx in developing communist ideology.—Ed.

16. Karl Marx, *A Contribution to the Critique of Political Economy* (New York: International Library Publishing, 1904), 11. [Bavinck gives the quotation in German: "Es ist nicht das Bewustsein des Menschen, das ihr Sein, sondern umgekehrt ihr gesellschaftliches Sein, das ihr Bewustsein bestimmt."—Ed.]

the final instance, economic factors are indeed the decisive factor and make history carry on as a natural process. Nevertheless, he, with Marx and all his followers, built up a great zeal for taking action in this natural process, in order to arrange the future society according to their ideas. When they judge the present society from on high, attacking capitalism in violent language, speaking with burning indignation about social miseries, and—without ceasing—denouncing exploitation [*uitbuiting*], lovelessness, and the injustice of the bourgeoisie, it is not an exact scientific but rather a moral judgment. It is ethics applied to the economy, which causes them to witness and act accordingly.[17]

Ideal norms, therefore, do not exist only in theory. They are not abstract concepts that subsist outside life and have some value only in the academy. They are factors of reality itself. They are the compass of our lives. In practice, they apprehend us in every moment. All people naturally do the things that are in keeping with the law and by this show that the work of the law is written on their hearts. If we do not arbitrarily and superficially limit reality to what we see with our eyes and touch with our hands, these norms are then entitled to an equally objective and unquestionable existence, just as the sensible

---

17. Ludwig Woltmann, *Der historische Materialismus: Darstellung und Kritik der marxistischen Weltanschauung* (Düsseldorf: Hermann Michels, 1900), 173, 206, 366; Heinrich Pesch, *Liberalismus, Socialismus und Christliche Gesellschaftsordnung* (Freiburg: Herder, 1901), 3:281; Pesch, *Lehrbuch der Nationalökonomie* (Freiburg: Herder, 1905), 1:309.

observations of nature are. With undeniable power, they establish in each consciousness, in head and heart, in reason and conscience, a witness of their existence. They grant existence to a series of moral phenomena and facts, consciousness of freedom, sense of duty, feeling of responsibility, self-incrimination, repentance, contrition, and so on that are as certain and stand as indisputably as the reality we perceive with our physical senses. And still there is more: they are the basis of law and morality, of life and labor, of discipline and punishment, of family and society and state, of science and art, of our entire culture. Take them away, and there is no truth, no science, no law, no virtue, and no more beauty. Nothing then remains for which life is worth living. Our humanity would then degrade into bestiality.[18]

This objective reality of logical, ethical, and aesthetic norms points back to a world order that can have its origins and existence only in God almighty.[19] In order to retain a place for faith in the majesty of the moral world order, Kant—with good intentions, no doubt—dug a deep gorge between theoretical and practical reason,

---

18. Otto Liebmann, *Zur Analysis der Wirklichkeit* (Strasbourg: Trübner, 1900), 587.

19. E. W. Mayer, "Über den gegenwärtigen Stand der Religionsphilosophie und deren Bedeutung für die Theologie," *Zeitschrift für Theologie und Kirche* 22, no. 1 (1912): 41–71, demonstrates, equally, that reliance on the logical, ethical, and aesthetical norms assumes religion and rests on belief in God's existence. Religious belief is "indeed the often overlooked and denied, and yet ready bearer of all true spiritual-moral culture" [*der zwar oft übersehene und geleugnete und dennoch vorhandene Träger aller wahrhaft geistig-sittlichen Kultur*]. There is no truth, science, [or] art without belief "in a binding order, in absolutely valid values" [*an eine verpflichtende Ordnung, an absolut geltende Werte*]. Heinrich Rickert, *Der Gegenstand des Erkenntnis: Einführung in die Transzendental-philosophie*, 2nd ed. (Tübingen: Mohr Siebeck, 1904), 71.

between science and morality (religion). If in respect of all transcendental things, science must end up with a *non liquet* ["it is not clear"], faith would get a free rein in this world. In fact, however, he has weakened his own position with this dualism. In the first place, science would not allow itself to be restricted in this way, and the world of moral phenomena soon adopted its evolutionary viewpoint. As such, when the world in its entirety taught him nothing about God, Kant was forced to look for the basis of morality in human nature and to make the human being into his own lawgiver.

If, however, the whole world, the entirety of nature and also of the human, as it pertains to his physicality, is reserved for a neutral science; if it is admitted that in that terrain nothing of a divine government can be detected but that a purely mechanical necessity rules, to stop then at the moral life in order to proclaim freedom there, and to borrow the postulate that God exists and that the soul is immortal, makes a feeble impression. Such dualism is not power but weakness. If God can be overlooked in the emergence and existence of the world, if even the moral world order derives its origin and existence from the human, then his existence is not necessary merely for the compensation of virtue and happiness. The dualistic worldview shortchanges both God and world, religion and science, judgments of "worth" [*Werth-*] and of one's "self" [*Seinsurtheile*]. It abandons the outside world to unbelief and the inside world to superstition. It breaks the harmony of *physis* and *ethos*, of becoming and acting, of knowing and doing, of head and heart.

If the logical, ethical, and aesthetic norms deserve absolute validity; if truth, goodness, and beauty are goods worth more than all the treasures of this world, then they cannot thank the human—for whom law was made—for their origins. There is only a choice to be made between the two: the norms of true and false, of good and evil, of beautiful and ugly emerged slowly in history by evolution, but they are not absolute, and while they are true and good today, tomorrow they may be untrue and evil; or, they have absolute and immutable being, but then they are not products of history—they merit a transcendent and metaphysical character, and because they cannot float in the sky, they have their reality in God's wisdom and will.

This same divine wisdom that thought and knew the world before she created it, that by this thinking granted reality to things and truth to our intellect, also determined the norms for our knowing, willing, and acting. The ideas that lay the connection between thinking and being, between being and becoming also provide harmony between becoming and acting, between *physis* and *ethos*, between knowing and doing, between head and heart. Because there is no polytheism, there is no different God before nature than the one before the moral world; next to the God of power, there is no other God of love. But it is the one almighty, true, and holy God who stands above all and reveals himself in everything, who created, sustains, and reigns over the natural and moral order. How different the natural, logical, ethical, aesthetic laws are; they—just like the various substances—have causes and forces that occur in creation; they have a common origin[20] and cannot, therefore, fight with each other. Through this unity, nature acquires a meaning and a value that it could not obtain by an atheistic or pantheistic view. Nature is no foolish, brutal, or demonic power but a means to the revelation of God's thoughts and virtues. Nature is an unfurling of his wisdom and a reflection of his glory. In defiance of all disharmony between virtue and happiness, the world is still a suitable place for the human being to live—not heaven but also not hell, not paradise but also not a wasteland, a domicile that corresponds with his present condition. Under the influence of Darwinism, the thought has emerged that this world was nothing other than a scene of struggle and misery. But this representation is as equally one sided as is the idyllic-nature view of the eighteenth century.[21] Scripture avoids both extremes; it rejects the optimism and the pessimism in their falsehood but after having first fully recognized the elements of truth that are hidden in both.

---

20. Liebmann, *Zur Analysis der Wirklichkeit*, 717.

21. Among others, Prince Kropotkin has repeatedly pointed out the one-sided character of the Darwinian view of nature. Alongside much competition and misery, much love, participation, and helpfulness can be seen in the natural world. Animals of the same species offer each other support in life. This factor is of great significance to the development of the world process, because through it, mutual goodwill, a sense of justice and fairness, indeed, of self-sacrifice, is advanced, and a [form of] social society is made possible in the animal and human kingdoms. See his essay "De ethische behoeften van onzen tijd," *Wetenschappelijke Bladen* (April 1905), 33–57. [Prince Peter Kropotkin (1842–1921) was an aristocratic Russian revolutionary philosopher.—Ed.]

And not only does the Christian worldview objectively restore the harmony between the natural and moral order, but through this it also brings about a wonderful unity subjectively between our thinking and doing, between our head and our heart. If the same divine wisdom grants things their reality, our consciousness its content, and our acting its rule, it must be the case that a mutual harmony exists between these three. The *ideae* ["ideas"] in the divine consciousness, the *formae* ["forms"], which constitute the essence of things, and the *normae* ["norms"], which have been put to us as the rule of life, cannot then struggle against each other but must be related as closely as possible. Logic, physics, and ethics are built on the same metaphysical *principia*. The true, the good, and the beautiful are one with the true being. And so head, heart, and hand, thinking, feeling, and acting also come together in recognition of their full rights and, at the same time, are protected from all kinds of exaggerations and excesses. Intellectual, mystical, and ethical elements hold each other in equilibrium, and Hegel, Schleiermacher, and Kant are reconciled with each other.[22]

The divine authority and the absolute legitimacy of the ideal norms, however, make us feel the deviation [from them]—which the human world shows us—all the more painfully. All people recognize that there is an awful distance between what ought to happen and what actu-

---

22. Willmann, *Geschichte des Idealismus*, 3:436, 494.

ally happens, between the demand and the fulfillment of the command. We are facing the mystery of evil that torments all, that has occupied the thinkers of every age, that has driven all religion and philosophy out in search of a way of redemption. If now the laws of our life are what they are, of divine origin and absolute validity, then their violation holds the highest serious meaning. There are thousands upon thousands who deem sin a minor issue, which they explain from matter, from the flesh, from the finitude and limitation of human nature and which they try to understand as a necessary moment in the course of human development. But whoever has beheld the majesty of the moral law can have no peace with these theories. There is but one view that allows sin to be what it really is and does not weaken its reality or its nature by reasoning, and that view is from Holy Scripture. Scripture does not flatter the human being but tells him what he must be according to God's law and what he has actually become through sin. Sin is "lawlessness" [ἀνομία], deviation, violating the law, backtalk from our will against God's will, "hatred of God" [ἐχθρα εἰς θεον]. It thus bears a profoundly ethical character. Among all religions, it is Christianity alone that views *sin* as strictly religious-ethical, detached from all substance, and distinguished from all physical evil.

But it is precisely the ethical nature of sin that grants it an affective seriousness. For if sin is a matter of the will and, as all profound self-knowledge teaches, is not just from some external, accidental willful acts but from the power of the will; if it is an idiosyncrasy and inclination of the will that is already present from birth, the path of "self-redemption" [*Selbsterlösung*] is entirely cut off for the human being. If the mind of the flesh is enmity against God, it cannot submit itself to the law of God. As the rule goes, *operari sequitur esse*, "function follows being," that being must first be changed before there shall be another kind of acting. If a tree shall bring forth good fruit, then it must first be made good. Kant and Schopenhauer[23] both perceived human nature's deep moral decay. They both recognized that moral evil rests *in* rather than simply *on* the human being; they both also therefore considered "a kind of rebirth" [*eine Art von Wiedergeburt*] necessary for liberation from evil. And yet they both became unfaithful to their starting point: Kant inferred, without any foundation, from the *must* to the *can*, as though the categorical imperative tells us that as we ought to be good, then we must also be able to be so (otherwise, the categorical imperative would be the most unreasonable thing in the world).[24] And Schopenhauer believed that the unfree, blind will, which is capable only of willing, can—by insight into the suffering of the world—recoil from its own work and "deny" [*verneinen*] itself.[25] And all those

---

23. Arthur Schopenhauer (1788–1860) was a German philosopher.—Ed.

24. Immanuel Kant, *Die Religion innerhalb der Grenzen der blossen Vernunft* (Leipzig: Voss, 1838), 41, 50.

25. Arthur Schopenhauer, *Die Welt als Wille und Vorstellung* (Leipzig: Brockhaus, 1887), 1:448.

who know of no salvation as a work of God must do this. If they are unbiased, recognizing sin for what it truly is, there remains no possibility of salvation for them. If they, on the other hand, hold fast to the possibility of salvation, then they are forced to deprive sin of the serious character that they had first assigned to it.

Once again, it is the Christian religion alone that reconciles this antinomy, that fully recognizes the moral decay and inability of human nature and yet opens to us a way of salvation. The salvation known by it, though, is not a human act but is only the work of God. The continued existence of the world, the history of the human race, the character of sin as something that should not be, the necessity of the idea that the good must triumph because of its absolute validity can lead us all to the supposition that there is a salvation. For why would creation continue to exist if it were not destined to be established through re-creation from out of its ruin? But if it is understood that salvation is nothing other than the work of God, it is evident that it can be known by us only through revelation, and then salvation must itself supervene in the world as such a work of God and be an ineradicable component in the history of our [human] race. The Scriptures teach us to understand salvation as such. This same divine wisdom that created the world also re-creates it, and this same divine energy that makes things that exist persist also leads them to a firmly established conclusion. The plan for salvation is sealed within the plan for creation. As creation, being a work of wisdom, points back to generation, it also points forward to revelation, which—starting immediately after the fall and developing historically—reached its pinnacle in Christ. Salvation presupposes revelation, and revelation has salvation as its goal, or rather, salvation is itself revelation breaking in from the hidden counsel of God and making itself a part of the history of humanity. Although revelation has this soteriological content, it is a restoration, and not an annihilation, of God's creative work, which was corrupted by sin. Revelation is a work of reformation. In re-creation, the creation is restored in all its *formae* and *normae*: the law in the gospel, justice in grace, the cosmos in Christ. That is why the Christian religion, as we come to know it from Scripture, is wholly at home in the world in which we live. Although the "causes" [*causae*] of this re-creation do not lie in forces given to the world in the work of creation, the Christian religion has nonetheless come into the world and fits within it like a key in its lock. Christ is from above, but he was born of a woman in the fullness of time and was born under the law. If sin is also an inclination of the will, if the moral law has absolute validity, if the good is directed—according to its idea—to triumph over all opposition, the religion that shall bring this triumph must be the wisdom and power of God, not only in word but in deed, not only in doctrine but in life; it must become flesh and blood in our race, and, as a work of divine energy, it must insert and maintain itself in the midst of the world.

The strivings of those who want to remove the necessary "truths of reason" [*Vernunftwahrheiten*] from the accidental "truths of history" [*Geschichtswahrheiten*], the idea from the fact, the concept from the observation, and who want, thereby, to turn Christianity into a philosophical system, are thus superficial. The religion that will save humanity from sin and bring it into mastery of the good must be "history" [*historie*]; it must exist in a series of divine acts that carry on from the beginning to the end of history. As such, salvation does not merely remain as an idea that floats above us, but rather, it is what it wills itself to be, and it brings about what it aims to accomplish. Christianity is not exclusively a teaching about salvation, but it is salvation itself, brought about by God in the history of the world. As a matter of fact, in all religions there is an awareness that faith and "history" [*historie*] coinhere. They all have their theogony and their cosmogony, their mythology and eschatology, and sometimes they elevate themselves to the notion of a world drama, of a powerful struggle between the realms of light and darkness. In Christianity, however, salvation is unleashed, on the one hand, on the whole cosmic process, and on the other, on the heart and soul, the core and essence of all world history. Here revelation begins in Eden, carries on through the centuries, receives its center in the person and work of Christ, and concludes with the end of the ages. Not only do the facts of this revelation support and illustrate our faith, and not only do they serve to prove that God reveals himself beyond us in nature and history [*geschiedenis*] and to protect our faith from individual caprice and counterfeit mysticism,[26] but they are also, according to the twelve articles in the Apostles' Creed, the object and content of our faith. For a Christian does not distinguish himself from those who confess another religion merely by way of his purer concept of God but by his faith in the living and true God, who created the world, who maintains and governs it, and in whom the world realizes salvation itself according to the counsel of his will.

There is no place for this wonderful work of re-creation in the fearful world system of mechanistic monism and historical materialism. Even more, these philosophies undercut not only revelation but also history, and it is not at all strange that many caught in the snare of the exact sciences deny any scientific and pedagogical value to history. Whatever right historical materialism may have in considering the influence of all sorts of external influences on the human being, ultimately no one accepts the result that history is nothing other than a mechanical process or a mathematical sum. The human is subject to external influences but also exercises influence. He is not passive in the face of the events but takes an active role

26. Karl Bauer, "Die Bedeutung geschichtlicher Thatsachen für den religiösen Glauben," *Theologisch Studien und Kritiken* (1904): 221–73.

in them; society is a requirement for but not the origin of personality.[27] Certainly, there is also a causal coherence in history [*geschiedenis*]; the law also applies there that out of nothing, nothing comes. But the "causes" [*causae*] that are at work here are much more complicated and numerous than in the fields of mechanics and chemistry. Alongside the physical causes of all sorts of nature, psychical causes emerge here: the intellect and the will, reason and the conscience, temper and passion, the heroic and the genius, all these factors that lie hidden in the personality. These causalities are in large part of such an intimate and mysterious nature that it is impossible to deduce events in the manner that one can draw a conclusion from the premises. Although psychology is indispensable for the historian, in the explanation of events he can never posit anything more than a stronger or weaker degree of probability and in the end always faces the mystery of personality. "The wholly original, only existing once, the ἅπαξ λεγομενον in the individual person stems from what is beyond comprehension."[28] And even if one rejects a free will that one can act fully arbitrarily and without motives, in the will a psychic causality is at work that differs from physical causes not by degree but in essence. The freedom of the will does not exclude causes but is

---

27. Rudolf Eisler, *Soziologie: die Lehre von der Entstehung ind Entwicklung der menschlichen Gesellschaft* (Leipzig: Weber, 1903), 55.

28. Liebmann, *Gedanken und Thatsachen*, 1:456. [Bavinck gives the quotation in German: "Das ganz Urwüchsige, nur einmal Vorhandene, das ἅπαξ λεγομενον in der Einzelperson stammt aus dem Unergründlichen."—Ed.]

opposed to all such causes that combat its own nature. Whether we understand this distinct nature of the will is another question, but it is a reality just as much as that of matter and force.

Moreover, the task of the historian is different from the task of the psychologist. If the historical researcher might first describe an event only if he had understood it psychologically, not only would he lose himself in details, he would also never come to the end of his research, not even to a single fact. Just as a judge very certainly must take into account the character of the criminal when defining the degree of punishment and at the same time must recognize a deviation from the law in the measure of his verdict, so the historian also must find out the causes of events, but by means of his research, he must try to come to knowledge of the idea that is embodied therein. History [*geschiedenis*] is there, in the first place, if the events are connected to each other; if they have a connection to general human (and therefore recognized, or at least known, by all) values; if they have had a positive or negative influence on economic, social, political relationships, on the artistic, literary, scientific, moral, religious aspirations of the human race; if they have brought forward the idea in its triumph over nature; if they have multiplied the ideal goods—the true, the good, the beautiful—and have enriched humanity.[29]

---

29. Ursul Philip Boissevain, *Wettelijkheid en Werkelijkheid* (Groningen: J. B. Wolters, 1904).

Christianity first granted such a view of history to us:

History meant far more to Christianity than it did to the ancient world. It was the Christian conviction that the divine had appeared in the domain of time, not as a pale reflection but in the whole fullness of its glory; hence as the dominating central point of the whole it must relate the whole past to itself and unfold the whole future out of itself. The unique character of this central occurrence was beyond all doubt. Christ could not come again and yet again to be crucified; hence as the countless historical cycles of the ancient world disappeared, there was no longer the old eternal recurrence of things. History ceased to be a uniform rhythmic repetition and became a comprehensive whole, a single drama. Man was now called on to accomplish a complete transformation, and this made his life incomparably tenser than it had been in the days when man had merely to unfold an already existing nature. Hence in Christianity, and nowhere else, lie the roots of a higher valuation of history and of temporal life in general.[30]

---

30. Eucken, *Geistige Strömungen der Gegenwart*, 190. Original German: "Dem Christenthum wird die Geschichte weit mehr als dem Alterthum. Mitten in die Zeit war nach seiner Ueberzeugung das Göttliche eingetreten, nicht in mattem Abglanz, sondern mit der Fülle seiner Herrlichkeit; als beherrschender Mittelpunkt des Ganzen musste es alles Vergangene auf sich beziehen und alles Zukünftige aus sich entfalten. Die Einzigartigkeit dieses Geschehens litt keinen Zweifel, nicht immer vom neuem konnte Christus kommen und sich kreuzigen lassen; so entfielen die unzahligen Perioden, die ewige Wiederkehr der Dinge; die Geschichte wurde aus einem gleichmassigen Ablauf von Rythmen ein zusammenhangendes Ganzes, ein einziges Drama; der Mensch ward hier zu einer völligen Umwandlung aufgerufen, seinem Leben dadurch eine unvergleichlich höhere Spannung gegeben, als wo es nur eine vorhandene Natur zu entfalten galt. So liegen die Wurzeln einer höheren Schatzung

Nevertheless, the Christian religion has not provided us with this rich view of history in such a way that it would be possible to preserve it [simply] by ignoring difficulties. But Christianity is itself the central content of this great history. If Hegel believed in reason and spirit in history and often—with brilliant insight—perceived the realization of divine thought in it, then that is a view of history that has been derived from Christianity but that also is disconnected from Christianity, that has lost its content and faded into an empty slogan. Just as the fundamental ideas of the Christian faith are supported by science and nature, they are much more so by history. Everyone who thinks it through must come to this insight: apart from and without Christianity there is no possibility of history in the proper sense, no history of the world and humanity. If the Christian religion, which has been prepared for by revelation from Eden onward and first reaches its goal in the second coming of Christ on the last day, if this religion is not the real redemption of humanity and re-creation of the world, all ground for the belief that history is development and progress, that

---

der Geschichte und des zeitlichen Lebens nirgend anders als im Christenthum." [English translation from Rudolf Eucken, *Main Currents of Modern Thought*, trans. Meyrich Booth (New York: Scribner, 1912), 246.—Ed.] Cf. Werner Elert, *Prolegomena der Geschichtsphilosophie: Studie zur Grundlegung der Apologetik* (Leipzig: Deichert, 1911); W. Lehmann, "Glaubensbetrachtung und Geschichtsforschung in ihren Prinzipien," *Zeitschrift für Philosophie und philosophische Kritik* (1912): 81–101; Albert von Ruville, *Der Goldgrund der Weltgeschichte: Zur Wiedergeburt katholischer Geschichtsschreibung* (Freiburg: Herder, 1912); see also the chapter "Openbaring en Geschiedenis," in my *Wijsbegeerte der Openbaring* (Kampen: Kok, 1908), 95–119. [For a modern English translation, see "Revelation and History," in *Philosophy of Revelation: A New Annotated Edition*, ed. Cory Brock and Gray Sutanto (Peabody, MA: Hendrickson, 2018), 92–116.—Ed.]

it strives for a goal and originates in the completed kingdom of God, falls away.

For that reason Christianity is not hostile to "history" [*historie*], but it is the animating idea, the leading thought, the all-pervasive leaven, in it. [Christianity]
gives it content and form, meaning and a goal. It makes
history what it is and must be. Science can stand only if
the theistic worldview, which lies at the foundations of
Christianity, is correct. Nature comes into its own and
receives its proper place only if it is just as the Scriptures
make it known to us. And history is true history only if
revelation not only illumines it but has itself also entered
into it historically and as such lifted it up to the heights
of its particular idea, to a work of God, to the genesis of
the kingdom of heaven. For just as ordinary human history exceeds nature, revelation also exceeds history. We
do not understand how divine causality is effective in the
creation by special revelation. Insofar as it concerns understanding, the degree of our humility can never be too
great. Apart from the fact that the human being is prone
to finding the measure of what *is* intelligible to be that
which he *finds* intelligible, it is false that science should
have to presuppose the intelligibility of the world.[31] For
there is a distinction between knowing [*kennen*] and understanding. We know the operation of chemical and
mechanical forces but do not understand them in their

---

31. Johannes Reinke, *Die Welt als That* (Berlin: Paetel, 1903), 7, 45, 64,
296, 327.

inner being. We know that in history there is another psychical causality at work and fathom, to some degree, the character of the human being, but the issue of the will remains unresolved both before and after. We believe in the immanent action of God in all creation through the ordinary path of his providence, but the nature of this working goes far above our understanding. The difference between the unlearned and scientific person exists, to a great extent, in that for the former, everything is [simply] obvious, and for the latter, everything becomes more of a wonder the longer it is considered. The problems we face with special revelation are, therefore, in principle not greater than those we face with general revelation and find within the sphere of the created. "The difficulty with which these effects of revelation can exist with natural causal connections is no greater than that of how the spiritual life can intervene in the natural, just as the will can be divided in the chains of natural mechanical causes."[32]

We know only this: that a worldview that does justice to the unity and diversity of the world leaves room for a special revelation and that to combat this as impossible can take place only from the standpoint of a mechani-

---

32. Richard H. Grützmacher, "Die Forderung einer modernen positiven Theologie unter Berücksichtigung von Seeburg, Th. Kaftan, Bousset, Weinel," *Neue kirchliche Zeitschrift* 15, no. 6 (June 1904), 451. Original German: "Die Schwierigkeit, wie diese Offenbarungswirkungen mit dem naturbedingten Kausalzusammenhange bestehen können, ist nicht grösser als die, wie das geistige Leben einzugreifen vermag ins natürliche, wie der Wille sich einzureihen vermag in die Kette der natürlich mechanischen Ursachen." [Cf. Richard H. Grützmacher, *Studien zur systematischen Theologie*, vol. 2, *Heft. Hauptprobleme der gegenwärtigen Dogmatik; Die Forderung einer modernen positiven Theologie* (Leipzig: A. Deichert, 1905), 94.—Ed.]

cal worldview, which would bring us to a loss of everything spiritual and ideal. The choice, then, is between one of these: the mechanical view is the right one, but then there is no place not only for miracle [*wonder*] but also for psychic causality, for reason and will, for conscience and freedom; or the organic worldview alone answers the diversity and richness of the world, and then there is space not only for the human personality but also for the sovereign and free influence of God in all his creatures.

According to this view, there are different substances and forces, different causes and laws. To the extent that the forces are differentiated, so the laws by which they work and the effects that they bring about are also distinct. There is no lawlessness; neither is there anything that ever happens without cause. There is order provided for everything because God is a God of order in all the domains of his creation. But the same laws do not apply for everything—these differ for nature and history, for science and art, and for law and morality, and particularly in the realm of religion, they bear a special character. Already in nature and history we cannot proceed without metaphysics: truth, goodness, and beauty lose their absolute character if they do not have their "archetype" [*Urbild*] in God. And still, it is religion, above all, that educates us of God and brings us into contact with him. Not one of the many psychological or historical theories of religion seems to be in any condition to explain its origin

or to understand its essence;[33] religion presumes the existence, the revelation, and the knowability of God.[34] And
even more so, in particular, it is the Christian religion,
in its Old Testament preparation and its New Testament
fulfillment, that makes a special revelation of God's love
known to us, without which [Christianity] cannot be explained or maintained. Whoever longs for proof of this
can also be informed in the present day by the Bremen
preacher Kalthoff,[35] who recently fought against liberal
theology in the name of a better historical method and,
for the sake of a free and autonomous religion, stood up
against the "Professors' Jesus, who looks quite different
in the one university than in the other"[36] and is nevertheless continually proclaimed to the people as the ideal
example, as the way, the truth, and the life.[37] Such a spe-

---

33. Karl Girgensohn, *Die Religion, ihre psychischen Formen und ihre Zentralidee* (Leipzig: A. Deichert, 1903).

34. Cf. my *Christelijke wetenschap* (Kampen: Kok, 1904), 75.

35. Albert Kalthoff (1850–1906) was a German theologian who associated with the Bremen-based "German Monists League" [*Deutscher Monistenbund*] and who denied that Jesus was a historical figure.—Ed.

36. Bavinck gives the quotation in German: "Professorenchristus, der auf der einen Universität wieder anders aussieht als auf der andern."—Ed.

37. Albert Kalthoff, *Das Christusproblem: Grundlinien zu einer Sozial-theologie* (Leipzig: Diederichs, 1903); Kalthoff, *Die Entstehung des Christen-tums: Neue Beitrage zum Christusproblem* (Leipzig: Diederichs, 1904); Kalthoff, *Was wissen wir von Jesus? Eine Abrechnung mit Professor D. Bousset in Göttingen* (Berlin: Lehmann, 1904). After the "historical Jesus" had proved fruit-less, another effort followed: the "mythological Christ," who would be formed syncretistically, from all sorts of Jewish, Greek, and Eastern elements. In his *Christusmythe* (Jena: Diederichs, 1909), Arthur Drews was à la mode for a while, but he has now had his day. On this debate, see H. M. van Nes, *Historie, mythe en geloof: Jezus Christus in de hedendaagsche Wetenschap* (Leiden: Brill, 1912); B. B. Warfield, "Christless Christianity," *Harvard Theological Review* 5, no. 4 (October 1912), 423–73; K. Dunkmann, *Der historische Jezus, der my-thologische Christus und Jezus der Christ* (Leipzig: Deichert, 1910); Franz Xaver Kiefl, *Der geschichtliche Christus und die moderne Philosophie: Eine genetische Darlegung der philosophischen Voraussetzungen im Streit um die Christusmythe* (Mainz: Kirchheim, 1911).

cial revelation, however, as that of which Holy Scripture speaks, is so little in conflict with nature that it prefers to give it its proper place and meaning. It is in conflict with the aprioristic, mechanical theory that many people are imposing on both nature and history in the present day but not with nature and history as they exist in themselves. Just as the causal connection in nature does not prevent the emergence of a different and higher causality in history, the causal connection in the human world does not exclude the emergence of divine causality in special revelation and does not prevent it from working in its own manner and according to its own law.

And that which is in complete agreement with the organic-causal worldview comes into the light even more clearly when we see it from a teleological standpoint. For the moral world order proclaims loudly to us that it stands far above nature in value: What does it benefit a man if he gains the whole world and forfeits his soul? Everything is subordinate to the triumph of the good, that is, to the glory of God's name. Just as nature and history teach us that the higher always takes the lower into its service, so the "final cause" [*causa finalis*] makes all "efficient causes" [*causae efficientes*]—mechanical and organic, physical and psychical—as instruments, subservient to its own realization. According to the organic-teleological worldview of the whole universe, it is the divine energy that subordinates all the forces of creation to itself. Along the path of general or special revelation, it breaks into all the joints of the created organism, maintains and governs it, and leads it to the established end. Therefore, we believe and do not despair. Sin does not break God's power but brings it to a richer revelation. The world plan presses on as a redemption plan. Although history shows us so much disorder and regress, it still moves toward Christ's future. God executes his counsel, and according to his promise, we expect a new heaven and a new earth in which righteousness dwells.

With this worldview, which our "reasonable religion" provides us, we stand diametrically opposed to the thought and aspiration of this century. However difficult it is to summarize this in one formula, some character traits can be identified within it. In the first place, it is noticeable everywhere and in each domain that there is a great dissatisfaction with what exists, with Christianity and church, with law and morals, with science and art, with the family, state, and society. In every direction there is a call to search for a new religion, a new dogma, a new morality, a new science, a new art, a new marriage, a new criminal law, a new society. The second peculiarity of modern life is that one everywhere seeks to go back to the last elements, to the original components, to the so-called positive, indisputable facts. In "epistemology" [*Erkenntnisstheorie*], then, [this means going back] to the very simplest (no longer assembled) perceptions; in nature [it is] to the atoms, or, while they exist only hypothetically, to the energies, in which the whole world can be solved; and in family, society, or state, [it means going back] to the individual, or (because these are also assembled) to the urges and instincts. And finally, the aspiration is to build a new, better world from these original elements. In science, only the simple sensations are described as fully reliable, but whether mechanically through the device that is the brain or out of need and for the sake of practical motives, from these sensations the human being builds up all sorts of representations, concepts, and worldviews that do not have correlates in reality but are necessary by virtue of the organization of the human mind. In the world as perceived by our senses, the energies are the last real components, behind which we cannot go further. Once again, however, by compulsion or necessity, the human being forms from these a world unity, a nature, which has no objective reality but has its existence only in the human mind. And finally, in ethics, it is the instincts that gradually gathered humans together into cohabitation in marriage and family, in society and state, and made them behave according to certain rules but without these institutions and regulations corresponding to any objective idea. Everywhere, then, it is the I [*ik*] that creates the not-I [*niet-ik*], the human who acknowledges no authority above and considers himself to be fully autonomous, nominalism that seeks to banish the last remnant of realism. It is by all means "the will to power" [*der Wille zur Macht*], the "*I want,*" that lifts itself up against the "You shall." Being bound to laws is felt to be coercive not only in religion but also in morality, in law, in the family, in society, in the state, even in nature and in science. To the modern autonomous person, to have to think of logical laws, to see nature as ruled by laws that are independent of it, and to recognize the truth as a power that stands above him and that lets itself be found only in a defined way seems to be unbecoming.

It is this autonomy and anarchy that the Christian worldview resists with all its strength. According to it, the human being is not autonomous but is always and everywhere bound to laws that were not devised by him but that are prescribed to him by God as the rule of his life. In religion and morality, in science and art, in family, society, and state, ideas are everywhere, norms above him, which mutually form a unity and have their origin and existence in the Creator and Lawgiver of the universe. These norms are the ideal treasures, entrusted to humanity, the basis of all social institutions. They are the foundation not only of our knowing [*weten*] and knowing about [*kennen*] things but also of our willing and acting. They have authority in the academy but also in life. They are the authority for our head and our heart, for our thinking and our acting. And while the autonomy of the human severs the bond between subject and object and thus in principle dissolves everything into chaos, it is theonomy, as the Scripture teaches us of it, that gives every creature its rightful place and provides its true meaning. Then nobody and nothing is isolated. No creature is autonomous, and no one may do what he wants, neither the man nor the woman, neither the parents nor the child, neither the government nor the citizen, neither the lord nor the servant. They are all bound to God's law, each person in his own way and place. And not by contract or arbitrary will, not through coercion or the necessity of emergency, but according to God's order they live and work together, and they are destined for each other and bound to each other. The divine thoughts and laws are the foundations and norms, the goods and treasures, the connections and organization of all creatures. To conform ourselves to that life, in intellect and heart, in thinking and acting—that is to be conformed to the image of God's Son most profoundly. And this is the ideal and destiny of the human being. In maintaining the objectivity of God's word and law, all Christians are agreed and should stand together unanimously in this age. The battle today is no longer about the authority of pope or council, of church and confession; for countless others it is no longer even about the authority of Scripture or the person of Christ. The question on the agenda asks, as principally as possible, whether there is still some authority and some law to which the human being is bound. That is the "reevaluation" [*Umwertung*] to which we are all witnesses; therein is the evolution taking place before our eyes. And in this struggle, every man of Christian profession should assemble under the banner of the King of truth.

That does not, however, take away the fact that among Christians, difference of opinion can exist, especially, besides on other points, about the way in which the objective truth must become our subjective property. In particular, Rome charges the Reformation, day after day, of being the actual origin of subjectivism and individualism, of autonomy and anarchy, which now apply to all domains. And Immanuel Kant, who first formally articulated this autonomy, is therefore called the philosopher of Protestantism by Roman Catholics.[38] But this claim, although supported powerfully by the left,[39] is nonetheless in direct conflict with history. Every unbiased judge will recognize that protesting in itself does not at all necessitate coming to a principle of autonomy. The prophets lived in continual protest against their people. Jesus protested in the name of the Law and the Prophets against the traditions of the elders, against human commandments. Whoever would attribute all protest to autonomy and anarchy would give a carte blanche to lies and injustice and must condemn all reformation as a devilish work. Everything comes to the question, In whose name and against what does the protest go forth?

---

38. Willmann, *Geschichte des Idealismus*, 2:574, 3:345, 400; Albert Maria Weisz, *Die religiöse Gefahr* (Freiburg: Herder, 1904), 40. Josef Müller, *Moralphilosophische Vorträge* (Würzburg: Ballhorn & Cramer, 1904), 30; Michael Glossner, "Kant der Philosoph des Protestantismus," *Jahrbuch für Philosophie und spekulative Theologie* (1907): 1. In particular, H. Denifle, in his tendentious historical work *Luther und das Luthertum*, vol. 1 (Mainz: Kirchheim, 1904), has received a worthy refutation [in the Netherlands] in Dr. H. H. Kuyper, *Het zedelijk karakter der Reformatie gehandhaafd tegenover Rome* (Kampen: Kok, 1912).

39. Friedrich Paulsen, "Kant der Philosoph des Protestantismus," in *Philosophia militans: Gegen Klerikalismus und Naturalismus* (Berlin: Reuther und Reichard, 1901), 31–83; Julius Kaftan, *Kant, der Philosoph des Protestantismus* (Berlin: Reuther und Reichard, 1904); Otto Flügel, *Kant und der Protestantismus* (Langensalza: H. Beyer, 1900).

And there is no doubt, then, that from the beginning the Reformation was a protest in the name of the word of Christ and his apostles against the deviations that had invaded the Roman church in the domain of life and doctrine. It was principally different from humanism, building a dam against the unbelief that continued to reach out further from Italy, and later, just as Rome did, it protested against the *Aufklärung* ["Enlightenment"] itself. This *Aufklärung*, which is not stronger and which won no larger a following in Protestant countries than it did among Roman peoples, is not to be explained from the Reformation but rather from an abandonment of the principles of the Reformation. Kant is, therefore, not to be mentioned in the same breath as Luther. They each moved in entirely different circles of thought. For Kant there is nearly nothing left of the great truths of Christianity, wherein Luther found his power and peace—as far as content, Kant's faith consisted in the trilogy of rationalism. Kant was the philosopher not of the Protestantism of the Reformation but of the *Aufklärung*; he was a kindred spirit not of Luther but of Rousseau.[40]

---

40. Compare Bruno Bauch, *Luther und Kant* (Berlin: Reuther und Reichard, 1904) and Ernst Katzer, *Luther und Kant* (Giessen: Töpelmann, 1910). The former view received indirect support from Troeltsch, insofar as he—in his *Protestantisches Christentum und Kirche in der Neuzeit* (1909)—distinguished old and new Protestantisms in Hinneberg's *Kultur der Gegenwart* (1907) and insofar as he saw the actual turning point of eras in the second, rather than in the first [of these]. This interpretation gave rise to broad discussions. See Horst Stephan, *Die heutigen Auffassungen vom Neuprotestantismus* (Giessen: Töpelmann, 1911). [Jean-Jacques Rousseau (1712–1778) was a Genevan philosopher and writer influential in the political, economic, and educational philosophy of the eighteenth century.—Ed.]

And yet the Protestant Christian's verdict on Kant will come out differently from that of the Roman in one way. Against rationalism and supranaturalism, which considered religious truth to be rationally demonstrable and held the assent that rested on such proofs for religious faith, Kant thought that a doctrine so rationally handled lost the character of religious truth and that the rational approval attached to it could not be true, saving faith. And in as much, Kant—in his own way—reinterpreted a thought that was, from the beginning, proper to the Reformation. Religion is no doctrine that can be rationally proved, the acceptance of which being more useful to the degree that it is more mysterious. Religion is also not a work, as though the duty that automatically rests on us could ever elevate our moral impotence and unlock a way of salvation. Neither is religion a romantic mood, an aesthetic affection of the heart, a means to the adornment of our human nature, as though God were there for our sake and we were not here for his sake. But religion is more. It is something different from and higher than all these things together. It is to serve God with all your mind, with all your soul, and with all your might, to make oneself a living, holy sacrifice pleasing to God; it is to trust unconditionally in God as the rock of our salvation and of our portion in eternity. The truth is objective; it exists independently of us. It does not direct itself toward us; we have to direct ourselves toward it. But just as the wisdom of God became flesh in Christ, so should the truth also enter us. In the path of freedom, it must become our personal and spiritual property; through a living and true faith, it must become constitutive of our thinking and doing and then spread outside us until the earth is full of the knowledge of the Lord. That is what the Reformation desired. And because in this mighty religious movement the Reformed confession spoke all this clearly, for us it is the purest of all and its worldview the one that suits the present age—with its high aspirations and tremendous distress—the best.

General Index

Scripture Index